A Far Glory

A Far Glory

The Quest for Faith in an Age of Credulity

Peter L. Berger

THE FREE PRESS
A Division of Macmillan, Inc.
NEW YORK

Maxwell Macmillan Canada
TORONTO

Maxwell Macmillan International
NEW YORK   OXFORD   SINGAPORE   SYDNEY

The Free Press
A Division of Macmillan, Inc.
866 Third Avenue, New York, N. Y. 10022

Maxwell Macmillan Canada, Inc.
1200 Eglinton Avenue East
Suite 200
Don Mills, Ontario M3C 3N1

Macmillan, Inc. is part of the Maxwell Communication
Group of Companies.

Printed in the United States of America

printing number

1 2 3 4 5 6 7 8 9 10

Library of Congress Cataloging-in-Publication Data

Berger, Peter L.
    A far glory : the quest for faith in an age of credulity / Peter L. Berger.
    p.   cm.
    Includes bibliographical references.
    ISBN 0-02-902930-9
    1. Faith.   2. Sociology, Christian.   3. Christianity and culture.
I. Title.
BV4637.B38   1992
234'.2—dc20
                                                    92-24946
                                                        CIP

For Diya,
whose smile renews the world

Contents

Part III
The Consequences of Believing

Prefatory Note

Theology, at least for me, seems to be like a disease that lies dormant for years and then breaks out again at more or less regular intervals. This book continues themes that I tried to deal with earlier in my books *A Rumor of Angels* (1969) and *The Heretical Imperative* (1979). I leave it to the reader to judge whether there has been any interesting progress in what I have to say on these matters.

The impetus for writing this book came with an invitation to deliver the William Belden Noble Lectures at Harvard University for the academic year 1991/92. Chapters 4 through 6 contain the text of these lectures. After finishing these, which constitute the core of the argument, I decided to write the rest of the book around them, so to speak. I want to thank Peter Gomes, minister of Memorial Church at Harvard, who issued the invitation. He is, of course, quite innocent of the dubious literary consequences of his generous gesture.

Two chapters have previously appeared in print as articles, more or less in their present form. The prologue was published under the title "Worldly Wisdom, Christian Foolishness" in *First Things*, August–September 1990. The excursus was published in the fiftieth anniversary issue of *Partisan Review*, volume 51, 1984. Permission to use them here is gratefully acknowledged.

This book, like everything else I have written over the last three decades, could not have been written without the critical support of Brigitte Berger (the adjective carries both its conventional meanings).

Part I

The Social Context of Belief

Prologue:
Amid Different Follies

T he focus of the following reflections is a passage
from the first chapter of Paul's First Letter to the
Corinthians:

> For the word of the cross is folly to those who are
> perishing, but to us who are being saved it is the
> power of God. For it is written [the reference is to
> Isaiah 29], "I will destroy the wisdom of the wise,
> and the cleverness of the clever I will thwart."
> Where is the wise man? Where is the scribe? Where
> is the debater of this age? Has not God made fool-

3

ish the wisdom of the world? For since, in the wisdom of God, the world did not know God through wisdom, it pleased God through the folly of what we preach to save those who believe.

For Jews demand signs and Greeks seek wisdom, but we preach Christ crucified, a stumbling-block to Jews and folly to Gentiles, but to those who are called, both Jews and Greeks, Christ the power of God and the wisdom of God. FOR THE FOOLISHNESS OF GOD IS WISER THAN MEN, AND THE WEAKNESS OF GOD IS STRONGER THAN MEN.

Very often passages of the Bible come to us from distant times and places that are difficult to imagine, let alone identify with. This difficulty is much less in the case of the Pauline Epistles. The late Hellenistic world out of which they come and to which they are addressed has a rather modernistic feel. This was a world of sophisticated cities—affluent, cosmopolitan, pluralistic, and more than a little libertine. Corinth, I suspect, would appear quite familiar if we were transported there by time machine: A port city, a provincial capital, bustling with commerce, with an ethnically heterogeneous population of diverse religious affiliations, endowed (among other things) with a flourishing sex industry. To be sure, the Christian community to whom Paul wrote was not exactly the upper class of the metropolis; in all likelihood, its members were mostly what we would today call lower-middle-class. But they too must have had a sense of being part of an important, worldly-wise center. They too, at least vicariously, partook of the "wisdom of the world." In that perspective, the Apostle must have appeared a very odd fellow indeed, and his message even odder. What he writes to the Corinthians makes it very clear that he was fully conscious of these appearances.

The historian Michael Grant, in the opening lines of his biography of Paul, calls him "one of the most perpetually significant men who have ever lived." This statement can be persuasively defended, not on the basis of some theological presupposition, but as a sober historical assessment. It was Paul who transformed an obscure Jewish sect into a universal faith that decisively changed the course of history. It is clear from the sources that he must have been an extraordinary individual—a man of great learning and intellectual brilliance, an inspired speaker, with an overpowering personality and (last but not least) awesome courage. Despite these qualities, which were certainly known to the Corinthian Christians, I doubt very much whether Paul impressed sophisticated people as an appealing character. To say the least, he must have embarrassed them. He was obsessed with his mission, unbending and endlessly aggressive in his religious views, absolutist and authoritarian in his dealings with others, and on top of that afflicted with a malady whose details we don't know, but which we may well imagine did not add to his social acceptability. We may reconstruct the adjectives and phrases used to describe him both at the cocktail parties of the Corinthian elite (if the latter was aware of him at all) and in the pubs where his petit bourgeois clientele would gather—"fundamentalist," "simplistic," "compulsive," "asking too much of sensible people," "never listening to the other side of an argument," "perhaps a little crazy"—in sum, something of a disagreeable fanatic.

It is also clear, however, that the main reason for embarrassment was not the man but his message. It was that message, the "word of the cross" preached by Paul, which struck both Jews and Gentiles as scandalous foolishness, as an offense against both the wisdom of the educated and the common sense of ordinary people. Of course, the wisdom and common sense of Paul's time are not our own, despite the affinities we may feel for the Hellenistic world. Consequently, to appreciate the outlandishness of Paul's message, we should perhaps "translate" these discrepancies into contemporary terms. Take anything which in your immediate milieu is taken for granted as scientifically established knowledge or as self-evident common sense—and then imagine your reaction to someone who confidently and aggressively proclaims the opposite.

Paul's "word of the cross," of course, is the core of the Gospel: That God came into the world in the improbable figure of a small-town carpenter turned itinerant preacher, who was executed as a criminal, despised and abandoned, dead and and buried—and who then, in a moment that transformed the whole structure of reality, rose from the dead to become the mightiest power in the universe and the lord of all human destinies. People, then as now, are relatively prepared to accept savior figures promising redemption from the ills of human existence. It is the "cross" part of the message that constitutes the "stumbling block," the "folly." It is that crucial motif in Christianity that theologians have called the *kenosis*, the humiliation of God: The same God who has all power, who created this world and all possible worlds, has taken upon Himself the form and the fate of an ordinary man, and indeed a man who suffered the most agonizing afflictions of betrayal, torture, despair, and death. No one, Jew or Gentile, would have been taken aback at a statement that the power of God is greater than that of men; Paul's scandalous proposition is that the *weakness* of God reveals His true power, including the power to triumph over sin and death.

The Jews of Paul's time were looking forward to the coming of the Messiah, a miraculous savior who would end the sufferings of God's people and institute a reign of perfect justice. The "stumbling block" to them was the truly outrageous proposition that the Messianic expectations of Israelite tradition were fulfilled by this Jesus of Nazareth, of whom they had either never heard or who, as far as they were concerned, had died an obscure death over ten years previously. Many of the Gentiles were accustomed to savior cults. Corinth, it seems, was not an overly religious place (commercial centers rarely are). Hans Conzelmann, a New Testament scholar, describes it as the "absolutely normal picture of a Roman Hellenistic city," but he does mention sanctuaries to Isis and Serapis, familiar divinities of the ancient world; we can be quite sure that other denominations had their local branches. They all worshiped very powerful beings—that, after all, is what gods and godesses are—and the more recently imported cults emphasized offering salvation, including the promise of eternal life, to their adherents. The "folly" to the Gentiles was, once again, the kenotic core of Paul's message—the utter degradation of the savior as the necessary precondition of his triumph. To be sure, there were other offensive aspects to the Christianity that Paul preached, but it seems probable that this was the most offensive.

The Christian community in Corinth probably contained people of both Jewish and Gentile backgrounds, and even after their conversion they must have been troubled by the discrepancies between the faith they affirmed and the assumptions of their culture. They must have suffered very much from what modern psychologists call "cognitive dissonance"—the painful disagreement between what we believe and what others maintain with assurance. As far as we know, human nature has not fundamentally changed in the course of recorded history. We may, therefore, assume that the Corinthian Christians did exactly what people in this predicament do today—namely, tried to *reduce* the dissonance. In the event, this meant finding some way to reduce the discrepancies between the Gospel and the culture, to somehow accommodate the Gospel to the "wisdom of the world" and thus to make it *less* "foolish." It is clear from Paul's letter that there were a number of heresies of which he disapproved in the Corinthian community. New Testament scholars disagree on just what these heresies were; however, many favor the belief that there were doctrines related to what later came to be known as Gnosticism, an ingenious synthesis between Christianity and various Asian redemption cults that went a long way toward de-emphasizing the kenotic dimension of the Gospel. Be this as it may, it is reasonable to surmise that the Corinthian heresies sought to reduce the offensive starknesses of the Christian message, to make it less of a "folly," more in line with conventional assumptions and values. In other words, Paul was confronted with an early form of *aggiornamento*, to use a modern Roman Catholic term, which means, literally, to bring Christianity up to date. Protestants use other terminology to recommend such accommodations to the spirit of the times—to make Christianity "more relevant," to get the Church "on the right side of history," and the like.

The Apostle deplores the presence of quarreling parties within the Corinthian Christian community, apparently divided by this or that interpretation of the faith. He names one group claiming allegiance to himself, another to one Apollos, another to Cephas, and one (with mind-blowing humility) simply asserting that they "belong to Christ." This group was perhaps the first in the history of the Church to declare itself the only "true Christians," as against all the others who, by the same token, are false or flawed Christians; one is reminded here of the use of the word "Christian" by a number of modern American denominations, some distressingly small in numbers. But, despite this, we have no difficulty empathizing with the Corinthians' doctrinal parties. There is, of course, the well-known Professor Apollos at MIT or Harvard, there is the celebrity intellectual Cephas who publishes in all the right magazines and is seen weekly on PBS; there are Apollonians, neo-Apollonians, and post-Apollonians in our midst—and there are foundations putting up impressive funds to support one or the other side in their quarrels. Each party claims to have the *Zeitgeist* by the tail, to be the most authoritative or perhaps the only mouthpiece for the "wisdom of the world." Most important, there are regiments of Christian teachers, clergy, and lay people who are working full-time to update the faith in terms of the latest Apollonian or Cephalian wisdom.

To put this in sociological terms: Every human society has its own corpus of officially accredited wisdom, the beliefs and values that most people take for granted as self-evidently true. Every human society has institutions and functionaries whose task it is to represent this putative truth, to transmit it to each new generation, to engage in rituals that reaffirm it, and sometimes to deal (at least in words) with those who are benighted or wicked enough to deny it. In most societies in history this has been a relatively easy matter, because there was only one set of beliefs and values, a unified and coherent worldview that everybody knew and that almost everybody took for granted. Modern societies, however, share with the Hellenistic world the complicating factor of pluralism: There are competing beliefs and values, there is more than one worldview. This pluralistic situation usually forces on people a certain degree of tolerance, but it also sharpens the cognitive dissonances and therefore introduces an element of fanaticism into the quarrel. This co-existence of tolerance and fanaticism is an important characteristic of contemporary America, but that is not something to pursue as yet. The point is that the various efforts by Christians to accommodate to the "wisdom of the world" in this situation become a difficult, frantic, and more than a little ridiculous affair: Each time that one has, after an enormous effort, managed to adjust the faith to the prevailing culture, that culture turns around and changes. W. R. Inge, the Anglican theologian, put it thus: "He who would marry the spirit of the age soon finds himself a widower." Recent Christian theology is well populated with bewildered and understandably resentful widowers.

Still, some beliefs and values are generally shared, and continue for at least a while (say, a few lifetimes), even in a situation marked by pluralism and greatly accelerated cultural change. Modern science has provided some basic cognitive assumptions of this type, and modern technology has ensured that they are internalized by the majority of people, who know little about science. Other beliefs and values are much more unevenly distributed—by class, education, ethnicity, and other factors. This is particularly so with moral and political values, which are much harder to establish by scientific methods and therefore depend more on social support. Thus a contemporary individual can afford to be much more relaxed about the proposition that the earth is indeed a globe or that appendicitis can be cured by surgery than about the moral position that abortion is or is not homicide, or the political position that the Reagan presidency was or was not a great positive breakthrough for American democracy. It follows that some views will be perceived as "folly" virtually every-where in society, while other views will be the accepted wisdom in one social milieu and utter foolishness in another.

Our pluralistic culture forces those who would "up-date" Christianity into a state of permanent nervous-ness. The "wisdom of the world," which is the standard by which they would modify the religious tradition, varies from one social location to another; what is worse, even in the same locale it keeps on changing, often rapidly. As each new theology comes along it should have a label attached to it that gives its proper place of application (say: "Use only with people who have had four years of college") and a terminal date for its applicability ("Stop using five years from date of is-sue"). Perhaps, for some individuals who have been chasing the *Zeitgeist* in this manner for a while, "folly" begins to seem like not such an unattractive option.

Of all the sociological indicators as to what people believe and take for granted, the most reliable is class. Put an individual behind a screen and tell me nothing about that individual's background except occupation and income (the major determinants of class) and I will be able to make a large number of predictions about this individual's beliefs (including religious and moral ones), political attitudes (including voting behavior), and lifestyle (including such allegedly private matters as sexual practices). Thus, for example, if you tell me that the individual behind the screen is a middle-in-come English professor, I will predict that he or she is likely to be unchurched, is politically liberal, votes Dem-ocratic, drives a fuel-efficient imported car, and is pro-choice. This prediction may well turn out to be false in a particular case: Remove the screen, and what comes out may be a deconstructionist from Harvard who is a fierce Evangelical and a fervent Republican who drives a used Cadillac from one pro-life rally to another. As a sociologist I cannot say that such a figure is impossible; I *can* say that this is *unlikely*. Conversely, if the individual behind the screen turns out to be a middle-income stockbroker, I would not expect him or her to be averse to churchgoing, a liberal Democrat, an environmentally oriented consumer, or much of a pro-choicer. And, once again, a different set of probabilities would apply to an individual whose occupation and income place him or her in the working class.

The upshot of these considerations is quite simple: *The "wisdom of the world" today always has a sociological address.* In consequence, every accommodation to it on the part of Christians will be "relevant" in one very specific social setting (usually determined by class) and "irrelevant" in another. Christians, then, who set out to accommodate the faith to the modern world should ask themselves which sector of that world they seek to address. Very probably, whatever *aggiornamento* they come up with will include some, exclude others. And if the *aggiornamento* is undertaken with the cultural elite in mind, then it is important to understand that the beliefs of this particular group are the most fickle of all.

Of course, there are *some* cognitive and normative assumptions that are found, even today, pretty much throughout society. (If this were not so, society could not hold together at all.) By their very nature, these are *not* beliefs and values that are politically "relevant": Political battles are about ideas and propositions that people do *not* have in common. As already mentioned, many of these society-wide assumptions derive from modern science and the everyday applications of science by way of technology. To that extent, the widespread notion that there is such a thing as a "modern worldview" and "modern man" has some validity. The question that religious people should ask themselves is philosophical rather than sociological: Even granting that modern science has given us new and often profound insights into reality and that modern technology has enormously increased our control over our lives, is it not possible that some very precious things have been lost in the process? I am not just thinking of the unfortunate by-products of our technologized world that we hear so much about today. I am thinking of *truths* that may have been lost in the process of modernization. Our ancestors didn't know about particle physics, but they spoke with angels. Let it be stipulated that through the knowledge of particle physics we have gained a new measure of *truth*. But could it be that we have *lost* a truth when our conversation with angels came to a stop? Are we, *can* we be so sure that the truths of modern physics necessarily imply the untruth of angels? I'm not sure at all; indeed, I'm strongly inclined to believe the opposite. In that case the Christian churches (and other religious institutions) would be paying a very high price for the "updating" of their tradition—the price being some precious truths that they were the last to hold onto.

When Paul spoke of the "folly" of the Gospel and counter-posed it to the "wisdom of the world," he was pointing to a cognitive aspect of God's *kenosis*, of God's abasement. In Christian preaching, and quite properly so, we more often hear of its *moral* aspect: Jesus came especially to the poor and the despised, to the margins of society, and he died as a criminal; and today too we are more likely to find him visible on the margins than among the rich, the powerful, and the respected. This is the morally revolutionary content of the "word of the cross," and, it seems to me, this shocking message has never been fully absorbed in all the centuries of Christian history. It continues to shake the foundations of all moral systems invented by men, it relativizes all social hierarchies, and in the final analysis it shows up the hollowness of all humanly constructed orders. But the "wisdom of the world" is part and parcel of every such order; the "folly" of the Gospel is, precisely, that it relativizes, puts in question, everything that passes for "wisdom" and everyone who claims to possess it.

Protestant theologians have described God's work of salvation as an *opus alienum*, an "alien work." By this term they meant to emphasize that our salvation is not in our own hands, that it is altogether God's doing. This stress, of course, was at the core of the Protestant Reformation, in its emphasis on the primacy of grace and its rejection of "salvation by works." This aspect of Christian faith does not concern me at the moment. Rather, I want to emphasize the *alienness* of the Christian message as a whole: this savior proclaimed in the Gospel is one who breaks into human reality like an intruder—unexpected, unrecognized, indeed unappealing. In this, the savior actually authenticates his divine provenance: The divine always manifests itself as that which is alien, *not* human, *not* part of ordinary reality. Rudolf Otto, the great historian of religion, spoke of the "totally other," which he claimed is the essence of religious experience. The same quality is intended by the term "transcendent"—the divine, wherever it manifests itself, goes beyond anything that human beings are familiar with. In this aspect of otherness, Christianity does not fundamentally differ from other religious traditions—after all, Christianity *is* one religion among others, so this should neither surprise nor trouble Christians. But the kenotic dimension of the Christian message adds an alien quality distinctively its own. This, precisely, is the "folly" that Paul spoke of.

If the Church gives up this "folly," it gives up itself and its very reason for being. This is why the pursuit of the "wisdom of the world" is finally so pernicious. It is not just that it is more or less futile, for the sociological reasons I mentioned, or that it is philosophically dubious. More importantly, if the Church (or, for that matter, individual Christians) give up the transcendent core of the tradition in order to placate the alleged spirit of the times, what is given up is the most precious truth that has been entrusted to the Church's care—the truth about the redemption of men through God's coming into the world in Christ.

We do not know what ideas divided the Christian community in Corinth, those followers of Apollos or Cephas. It would be interesting to know and perhaps future New Testament scholars will be able to identify them. But it matters little as far as the main message of the Apostle is concerned. Similarly, an understanding of the various doctrines and ideologies that divide us today is interesting; on a certain level, such as that of politics, this may even be important or morally urgent. But in the face of the Gospel, which points us toward eternity, these distinctions are quite unimportant, indeed irrelevant. The Gospel is not of this world, and to try and make it so is to lose the redemptive power it contains.

I recently spoke with a sociologist in Spain who has studied the great changes that have occurred in the Roman Catholic church since the Second Vatican Council. He said something that struck me as very insightful. Christians who consider themselves "progressives," he said, always tell us to "read the signs of the times"; then he asked: Has it never occurred to these people that they might *write* some of these signs? At least in recent years, the stance of thinking Christians (and by no means only Roman Catholics) in the face of the "wisdom" of the modern world has been largely passive, even supine—a "reading" rather than "writing" attitude. The Gospel was subjected to the judgment of this or that worldly standard; rarely did the reverse occur. To be sure, there are all sorts of Christian orthodoxies and fundamentalisms around, and in America, at any rate, they have done very well. But they have *not* done well among those who are respected as thinkers and teachers of the Church. I'm not for a moment suggesting that it would be better if they had; the very last thing I want to advocate is some sort of fundamentalism or even orthodoxy. I *am* suggesting that there is a middle ground between the "progressive" surrender to the age and the fundamentalist denial of it. The first *only* "reads," the latter *only* "writes." Or, to change the image, the one listens and has nothing to say, the other speaks without having ever listened. It seems to me that Christian wisdom must always comprise both attitudes.

The preceding pages contain, in a nutshell, the position taken throughout this book in the matter of religious faith today. On the one hand, it is a position that does not fit easily into any of the officially defined camps. On the other hand, I do not flatter myself by thinking that this position is altogether original. It seems that there are many people today who do not fit into the available camps, and for reasons that may not be terribly different from mine. I don't look upon myself as a voice crying in the wilderness. I even think that I may have an audience out there. If I did not, needless to say, there would be little point in writing this book.

The position I will elaborate in what follows begins with a deliberate acceptance of the social context of one's struggles for truth and identity. In my own case, there can be no doubt that this has something to do with the fact that I am a sociologist which, after all, means looking for the social context of any human action or thought. But being or becoming aware of one's location in time and space, in history and society, is not the sole prerogative of sociologists. It is, I think, something that sooner or later occurs to any reflective individual. What this means more specifically today is the acceptance of the fact that we live in the modern world and that we are modern people. As I will spell out in some detail later, this emphatically does *not* mean that we must look upon modernity uncritically, that some alleged modern worldview becomes the yardstick by which any proposition about reality is to be assessed, or that we are obligated to strive for some ideal of being modern in our own lives. Much more simply, it means that one does not deny the situation in which one finds oneself.

There are people (and not only theologians or religious believers) who deny that there is any social context to their lives, and others who reject modernity. I believe that the denial is less than honest and the rejection misguided if not futile. Accepting our social context means today acknowledging the fact that the certainties of a traditional, pre-modern or non-modern society are not available to us. If we are concerned with truth, we will somehow try to push on from that recognition. This is not easy, but it is much better than denying the situation from which we must start. Of course it is possible to reject modernity, whether all of it or parts of it. There is even a rather heroic quality about such a stance, as individuals or entire communities try to live their lives and to think in deliberate defiance of powerful forces around them. I'm thinking here, for example, of the First Vatican Council, convened in 1870 just as the forces of modernity, embodied in the army of the new Italian state, were about to storm into Rome. In defiance of everything fashionably viewed as progressive and intellectually correct, the Council solemnly proclaimed the two dogmas of the immaculate conception of Mary and of the infallibility of the pope—each one a robust slap in the face of modernity. One need not believe in either dogma to appreciate the gesture. Heroism, however, brings no privileged insights; heroes can be dreadfully wrong. The position I take here accepts modernity, not only because it defines our context, but more importantly because it has yielded perspectives on the world and on the human condition that I hold to be true. Among these is the inevitably relativizing viewpoint of the modern historical, psychological, and social sciences. To use one of my own sociological phrases, this perspective recognizes that reality is socially constructed, and therefore that truth over and beyond these social constructions cannot easily be attained. What is more, I do not deplore this conclusion. I believe that it opens up fresh new approaches to the question of truth, in religion as in other matters. As I have suggested a few pages back, this aspect of our social context is surprisingly similar to the situation of the early Christians, who also lived in a quasi-modern world of competing faiths.

The modern pluralistic situation creates anxieties and tensions. It is possible to escape from them in opposite directions. One escape is into a false certainty, the other into an attitude that despairs of any possible access to truth. Both forms of escape are represented plentifully all around us today, with the representation of each varying somewhat by social milieu. Every type of orthodoxy is marketed with the promise of renewed certainty: "Come and join us, and you will know the truth, the way to live and, best of all, you will know who you really are." Of course there are secular orthodoxies as well as religious ones—not to mention scientific, political, aesthetic ones, and many others. In the area of religion it is fairly clear from sociology-of-religion data that, contrary to the expectations of many theologians and church leaders, it is precisely the groups that exude certainty, insist on strict doctrines, and make difficult behavioral demands to which people flock in large numbers. By contrast, religious groups that admit uncertainty and are lax in doctrine as well as codes of behavior have difficulty retaining their members let alone acquiring new ones. There is no psychological mystery about this. The uncertainties of modernity are burdensome; it is a great joy to be relieved of them. If one can bring oneself to surrender to the certainty offered by this or that orthodox community, religious *or* secular, then the joy will be quite intense. I find myself unable to accept any of these offers; I do not pass judgment on those who do accept; I do allow myself a measure of skepticism as to the ingenuity of their acceptance, if they are modern people.

On the opposite pole of possibilities there is the other escape into some form of nihilism or utter relativism, which either denies the very notion of truth in religion or our capacity to attain any measure of it. This too is liberating in its own way, because it too takes away the burden. It does so by denying that there is a burden to begin with. If there is no objective truth "out there," if religious affirmations are nothing but subjective exclamations about which it is senseless to argue, then there really is no burden there at all. Perhaps, if I'm told persuasively that there are no apples anywhere in this world, I might get over my curious craving for this imaginary fruit. But even if it were conceded that, somewhere "out there," religious truth might exist, if it is then asserted that there is no chance whatever of getting even a glimpse of it, then too there is some relief. Yes, I may have a sickness, but if there is absolutely no cure for it and if it has been established that I can somehow live with it, then I can relax in a way. I understand this very well, but this too is a direction in which I'm not prepared to move. I believe that the notion of religion as being nothing but an expression of human realities and needs is mistaken. And while I know all too well how difficult it is to make any religious affirmation with a measure of confidence, I'm also not prepared to give up the effort.

I suppose this could be described as a middle position. I have not invented it. It has been characteristic for some two hundred years of an important stream of religious thought and life, that of liberal Protestantism. I have long identified with this tradition, albeit with some reservations here and there. The argument of this book can fairly be characterized as a liberal Protestant one. However, it seems to me that the argument will be accessible to readers who have no personal affinity with liberal Protestantism, who belong to other Christian or non-Christian communities, or who have no clear religious identification at all. This is because there are important commonalities in the situations of people who try to reconcile a religious quest with an honest recognition of their contemporary social context. Such people may be Christians, Jews, Muslims, Buddhists, or agnostics. Obviously, if they follow my argument, they will want to reformulate it in terms of their own experiences and situations, but I think that they will not feel excluded from it. To be a believer, or even *to try* to be a believer, and nevertheless to reject as illusory the certainties held out by the orthodox: To take such a position, I think, brings with it problems and aspirations that are similar regardless of one's particular starting point. Among the problems is the moral one: How, given this religious position, can I act responsibly in the world? Among the aspirations will be the desire to belong to some visible community, and this leads to yet another common problem: Given this religious position, where can I find a community in which people like me can be at home? I will have something to say about these problems toward the end of the book.

Immanuel Kant was right when he maintained that the ultimate question in all of human thought is the question of "who am I?" Modernity has introduced a new uncertainty on this too. Certainty about one's true identity becomes as difficult to achieve as certainty about the ultimate reality of the world, and for the same reasons. Once again, it is possible to escape from this uncomfortable situation either into a false certainty or into a denial of the very possibility of an answer to the question of who I am. And once again I will take a middle position, somewhere between an orthodoxy of the self ("*this* is who you are, and nothing else") and a denial of quest as well as question ("there is no true self"). The sharpest formulation of this problem that I know in modern literature is in the work of the great Austrian novelist Robert Musil, which is why I have devoted a chapter to him. I have called it an "excursus," signaling that anyone with no taste for Central European *Angst* can safely skip the chapter without losing the thread of the argument. In the end, as I see it, the problems of religious belief and of the true self collapse into each other: Only within a religious view of reality can there be an answer to the question about the true self. Put differently: If I have a true self, it is that self which is God's project.

Finally, let me make some observations about the implications of all this for those of us who are indeed "scribes," members of that class which makes its living from producing and distributing what passes today for officially certified "wisdom." Much of what I have said here could be taken as a put-down of this class; to the extent that I belong to it, I could even be suspected of masochism or self-hatred. I would like to correct this impression. There is, to be sure, an element of put-down here: I intend to put down the arrogant delusion of intellectuals that they are superior human beings and the even more dangerous idea that, by virtue of these superior qualities, they constitute a moral or even political elite. These misguided notions are thoroughly un-Christian, but it seems to me that we don't need Christianity to instruct us on the foolishness of such pretensions—a realistic look at the world will do. Intellectuals do not have better moral judgment than people with little or no education, they do not live more wisely, they are certainly not more compassionate, they have not fewer but *different* superstitions, and they are capable of the most mindless fanaticisms. To say these things, however, is not for a moment to idealize or to romanticize those other people with little or no education. The ignorant, the poor, the underclass are not morally superior either (and it is not because of their superiority that Jesus preferred their company), they do not have deeper insights into life, their values and opinions have no privileged status. The "word of the cross" is radically egalitarian, *not* in a political sense, but in the infinitely more profound sense that before God all human pretensions are equally shown up to be as nothing.

Later on in this Epistle Paul speaks of different Christian vocations, all important for the community. "Scribes" are not mentioned, though "teachers" are, and those who "interpret." Whatever these titles may have meant in the Corinthian context, I believe that

there exists a legitimate intellectual or academic vocation—that is, of teaching and perhaps adding to the
manifold bodies of knowledge that constitute the "wisdom" of our modern world. This vocation is to be ex-
ercised responsibly and honestly, and it may be respected for that. It bestows no moral or political
privilege, not in society at large and certainly not in the
Church. This is not the appropriate occasion to develop
my understanding of the role of intellectuals in our society, but I did want to clarify that a put-down of the
pretensions of intellectuals in no way implies a rejection
of the intellectual vocation.

At the end of the day, the "word of the cross" is
addressed to all of us, whatever our vocation or our life
situation. Jesus preferred to move on the margins of society, but he is able to appear in every social location.
The "word of the cross" saves us because it tells us that
we don't have to be strong in order to participate in
God's power. God reveals himself in weakness, also in
our weakness—in social weakness, in moral weakness,
and also in intellectual weakness. He moves among the
poor, among sinners, among "fools." Once we have
had our various pretensions debunked, there is very
great comfort in this message.

Our attention here is directed toward God's weakness—His coming into the world in the weak form of a
man, this man's persecution and degradation, his
lonely despair and his painful death. In contemplating
God's weakness and Jesus' Calvary we inevitably include the weakness and the suffering of all creatures, in
the words of the Book of Common Prayer "all those
who are any ways afflicted, or distressed, in mind,
body, or estate" (and, of course, especially those whose
pain or sorrow has touched our own lives). If that were
all there is to Christianity, it would be the most doleful

religion, a truly masochistic and downright pathological belief. Of course, that is not the case at all. Lent is the prelude, not the culmination. Lent leads up to Easter, the ultimate weakness of God to the blinding revelation of His omnipotence. The "word of the cross" culminates and finds its true meaning in the word of the resurrection—Christ's resurrection and our own. It is this redemptive word that Paul carried with him on his restless travels and that he was anxious to protect against the false wisdoms of the world. The same redemptive word is the only reason for being of the Christian Church today, as it is the beginning and end of our faith.

1

Secularization and Pluralism

I t has for a long time been a widely accepted view
that the modern age brought about a steep decline
of religion both on the public scene and in the minds of
individuals. To say that this view has been widely accepted may even be an understatement; in some quar-
ters (as, for instance, among people with higher education) it has attained the status of a taken-for-granted
truth about which it would be silly to argue. The commonly used term for this alleged process of religious
decline is "secularization" and the theoretical elabora-
tion of it, by historians or social scientists, is called "sec-

25

ularization theory." Among the most fervent adherents of this theory have been theologians, many of whom, for at least a hundred years, have started with the unexamined assumption that modern man is unavoidably and irreversibly a secularized character, and that theology must come to terms with this alleged fact. Needless to say, this has not been a happy assumption for theologians. It has put them in the unenviable position of someone proclaiming the joys of sex in a community of the impotent, or of music among the deaf.

There has also been widespread agreement on the cause of the phenomenon. The culprit in this metaphysical road accident of modern history is generally taken to be science, more specifically *modern* science, which has radically transformed the conditions of human existence for the last few centuries. The secularizing effect is seen as having a double character, on the level of the mind by the inculcation of highly rational modes of thinking and on the level of practical living by the application of equally rational techniques to solve problems which previously rendered human beings helpless. If the scientist and the engineer are taken as typical figures of the modern age, it can then be said that religion has become unthinkable for the first and unnecessary for the second. The prior assumption, of course, is that religion is based on the incomprehensibility of the world and on man's helplessness in that incomprehensible world, so that it must necessarily decline as do these two conditions. The most evocative phrase to describe the resulting situation has been Nietzsche's "death of God." It is important to stress that quite different evaluations have been made in the wake of this diagnosis; some have deplored it as a terrible impoverishment, others have hailed it as a great liberation from superstition and as an essential precondition for progress.

As is usually the case with conventional wisdom, this view of things is partially valid. There can be no doubt that something like secularization has been occurring in parts of the world (especially in the West, where the view originated) and that it has been related to the historic process of modernization, or the transformation of human life brought about by science and technology. It can be shown that in various places, the advance of modernity has coincided step by step with a sharp decline of both religious practice and belief. Sometimes this decline occurred in a particular locality as the forces of modernity came to be established; at other times it can be observed as an accompaniment of migration. Thus E. R. Wickham (*Church and People in an Industrial City*) studied how Sheffield, one of the centers of British industrialization, saw its churches progressively emptied in the nineteenth and twentieth centuries as the new industrial society transformed the relation between religion and various groups in the population (first in the working class, then in the middle classes). Thus Gabriel LeBras, the founder of so-called "religious sociology" in France, studied the effect of migration from rural areas of the country to that vortex of modernization that is metropolitan Paris. There is an eloquent formulation in LeBras' generally pedestrian prose. In a study of migration from Normandy (possibly the most conservatively Catholic region of France) he wonders whether there might not be a magical piece of pavement in the Gare du Nord (the railway station where one would normally arrive in Paris from Normandy): As soon as one steps on that pavement, it seems, one is transformed from an observant Catholic into a person who never attends mass and who has seemingly lost all interest in religion. Of course, neither Wickham nor LeBras believed in some sort of secularizing magic: The reason for secularization in both instances is the transforming power of modernity.

The conventional view is also almost certainly correct in pointing to science and technology as secularizing factors. While it is true that many scientists have been very religious persons, it is also true that modern science fosters a mindset that is impatient of mystery and that seeks rational explanations in place of supernatural causalities. Since there are relatively few scientists, the effects of modern technology are probably more important as a secularizing force. Not just the engineer but anyone who employs modern technological machinery becomes accustomed to highly relational and pragmatic approaches to all the problems of everyday living. Since increasingly this includes virtually everyone, at least in advanced industrial societies, it is safe to conclude that this rationalization of the life-world will have very far-reaching consequences, on religion as on everything else. It is therefore plausible to see a connection between the "death of God" and the progress of modern industrial production as well as the consumption of its products.

So far, so good. Yet a theory that sees secularization as inextricably linked with modernity runs into serious difficulties. For one thing, there is the intriguing occurrence of secularity in situations long before the advent of modernity; the high culture of China may be the most important case (though some Chinese scholars would dispute this). Much more important, there are vast regions today in which modernization has not only failed to result in secularity but has instead led to reaffirmations of religion. The Islamic world today seethes with such reaffirmations. It would appear that the relation between religion and modernity is somewhat more complicated.

Max Weber, who did not use the term "secularization," spoke of "the disenchantment of the world." A wonderfully suggestive phrase: Human beings, passing from the enchanted garden of primeval religiosity into the cold comfort of modern reality. Modern scientific thought places man in a universe devoid of supernatural presences and modern technology gives him the limited comfort of increasing his control over the universe, limited because it cannot ever change the root circumstances of human finitude and mortality. It is no disparagement of Weber to say that he did not sufficiently perceive the possibilities of a *re*-enchantment of the world, precisely because the disenchanted world is so cold and comfortless. Thus, while the modern age has indeed been the scene of massive secularization, it has *also* been the scene of powerful movements of counter-secularization. Some of these movements have occurred within the boundaries of traditional religions—"revitalization movements," as anthropologists have called them. An example is the Ghost Dance, a violent movement in which the nineteenth-century American Indians reaffirmed their traditional identity. Yet others have taken new, non-traditional forms, and some have appeared in contexts that at first did not seem to be religious at all (the so-called "counter-culture" of the 1960s is a recent example). To paraphrase Mark Twain, the reports of God's death have been greatly exaggerated. It should be pointed out, of course, that this observation in no way constitutes an argument for the existence of God. It may be true that the reason for the recurring human outreach toward transcendence is that reality indeed includes transcendence and that reality finally reasserts itself over secularity. But it may also be true that religious resurgences occur for psychological rather than ontological reasons: Reality is indeed cold and comfortless, but human beings seek comfort and, again and again, they will be prepared to embrace comforting illusions.

Another exaggeration may have been the conventional view of the reach of scientific rationality. One does not have to look at religion only in order to find this thought plausible. It is amazing what people educated to the highest levels of scientific rationality are prepared to believe by way of irrational prejudices; one only has to look at the political and social beliefs of the most educated classes of Western societies to gain an appreciation of this. Just one case: What Western intellectuals over the last decades have managed to believe about the character of Communist societies is alone sufficient to cast serious doubt on the proposition that rationality is enhanced as a result of scientifically sophisticated education or of living in a modern technological society. Again, this observation does not necessarily lead to the conclusion that all the assumptions made in the conventional view about scientific rationality were altogether false. What the conventional view overlooked was the human capacity for what one might call creative schizophrenia: A nuclear physicist, for example, who would never write a sentence in a scientific article without carefully checking and rechecking every piece of evidence, will make dogmatic assertions about political matters based on no evidence but blind faith in a movement or regime into which this individual has projected some quasi-religious hopes.

But the most serious difficulty for the conventional view of secularization comes from the simple facts about religion in the contemporary world. Again, it would be wrong to propose that these facts conclusively falsify everything that has passed under the category of secularization theory. But they strongly suggest that the situation is more complicated.

There is indeed one geographical region and one cross-national group of people where secularization theory appears to apply very well. The region is Europe, and the group are people with Western-type higher education everywhere. There are no signs as yet of any counter-movement in the region; in many parts of the world there are strong counter-secularizing forces among Western-educated people. Northern Europe, probably beginning with England, has indeed undergone a process of secularization that can be correlated fairly accurately with the advance of modernity. Since the industrial revolution began in England, it fortifies secularization theory if that country can also be seen as the one in which that process began. Scandinavia in general and Sweden in particular represent the contemporary high points of secularization, both in terms of behavior and of expressed beliefs. What is interesting is that the same process of secularization appears now to have overtaken Southern Europe, notably Italy and Spain. At this point there is no evidence of counter-formations to this pervasive secularity. It remains to be seen whether the situation is any different in Eastern Europe. The question here is whether the recent importance of the churches in some countries (such as the Catholic church in Poland and the Lutheran church in the former German Democratic Republic) does indeed signify a revitalization of religion, or whether it was simply due to the absence of other institutions capable of providing a measure of "free space" in these totalitarian societies. In any case, Europe continues to be the prime example in support of secularization theory. Cross-nationally, there is a (rather thin) stratum of

Western-educated people—intellectuals, if you will—who appear to fulfill the predictions of secularization theory. One could call them "elective Swedes." Thus an individual can move around all over the world in the locales shaped by this stratum—universities, media centers, literary conferences, and so on—and be reasonably assured that he will not be assailed by religious voices. Such an individual might well think that this is what the whole world is like. He would be much mistaken. (Salman Rushdie is one individual who made this mistake, at great cost to himself.)

On the contrary, the rest of the world is as furiously religious as ever, and possibly more so. There is, first of all, the tenacious hold of traditional religion on vast numbers of people in almost all non-Western regions—in East and Southeast Asia (with the possible exception of Japan), intensely so in South Asia, and across the Muslim world, sub-Saharan Africa, and Latin America. Thus an individual in a village in India may have had a measure of modern education, perhaps be literate and have some knowledge of English, and use a variety of modern technological gadgets—and, nevertheless, live in a world totally dominated by the mental and behavioral structures of traditional Hinduism. More damaging to secularization theory, his cousin, a graduate of a Western-style university—and, say, a practicing nuclear physicist—may recently have joined a passionate movement seeking to re-Hinduize India, through bloodshed if necessary. The latter case implies resurgence rather than tenacity. Such resurgences are occurring throughout the non-Western world, some characterized by very great power to shape events. They are inadequately (and pejoratively) described by the term "fundamentalism," but whatever one calls them, they make it very difficult to argue that modernization and secularization are inextricably interlocked. Thus modern communications media (radio, television, audio- and video-cassettes) are today the principal vehicles for the dissemination of fiercely traditional religious messages, and a modern scientific education seems to provide little if any immunity against their appeal.

If one looks for revitalizing religious movements on a global scale, two stand out. One is Muslim, the other Evangelical Protestant. They have some psychological similarities, but their social consequences and respective relations to modernization are very different. The similarity is, of course, that both are reactive counter-formations. What they react *to* are the displacements and discontents of modernization. They also evoke a similar intensity of commitment on the part of those who join, and display an expansionist, missionary spirit. There the similarity stops; more of this in a moment. The point to stress first is the vast geographical scope and sheer size of these movements. Muslim revitalization movements have spread rapidly throughout the Islamic world, from the Atlantic Ocean to the China Sea, wherever the voice of the *muezzin* is heard in the call to prayer. The Iranian revolution has focused world attention on this phenomenon; and it is now very clear that the Iranian case is neither unique nor typical. Powerful Islamizing movements have appeared elsewhere, from North Africa to the southern Philippines, and many of them bear little resemblance to the Iranian case. The Evangelical movement, most of it Pentecostal in expression, is of even wider geographical scope. It is very powerful in East Asia, and enormously so in South Korea (Japan, again, is the exception). It has become strongly established in the South Pacific. It has also been very successful in sub-Saharan Africa, where it is often conjoined in highly unorthodox ways with resurgences of traditional African religiosity. Most dramatically, Evangelical Protestantism has been sweeping across Latin America with the power of a prairie fire, gaining vast numbers of new adherents (estimates suggest some 40 millions) and in some countries of the region—notably in Central America, in parts of Brazil, and in Chile—creating a powerful new social, political, and economic reality.

The two movements have very different relations with modernity, though both can be described as reactions to it. Neither relation lends much comfort to secularization theory. The Muslim movement is indeed neo-traditional—if you will, "reactionary"—both religiously *and* socially. The continuity between its religious and social contents is probably rooted in the very nature of Islam: One cannot accept its religious message without thereby implying a reconstruction of society. The hypothesis, then, suggests itself that Islamic revitalization is counter-modernizing both in its intentions, which are to return society to the rule of Islamic law, *and* in its real consequences, which pose a major obstacle to modern development. By contrast, the Evangelical movement is only partially counter-modern in its intentions, while it can be plausibly argued that its consequences are positively modernizing.

The reasons for this difference can be readily understood if one asks a simple question: Stipulating that both movements are "conservative," in the sense of looking back to an earlier and presumably better period of history, *which* period are they looking back to? In the Muslim instance, one would clearly designate the golden age of Islam—somewhere between Muhammad and the maximum expansion of the Arab empire; this would focus on a period between the seventh and the ninth centuries of the Christian era—that is, a period centuries before the onset of modernization. Evangelicals don't really have a golden age, unless it be the age of the Apostles, and they are not proposing that people today should go back to that. But if one asks in which period the values they propound were most firmly established in the Christian world, one would probably identify the eighteenth and early nineteenth centuries. The difference is not simply a matter of a thousand years; it is also the difference between "medieval" and "early modern." But these "early modern" values and lifestyles were very important vehicles of modernization, as Max Weber originally showed in his analysis of the so-called "Protestant ethic" and its role in the genesis of the modern world. The evidence concerning contemporary Evangelical Protestantism strongly suggests that it is playing a very similar role today (I would refer here to David Martin's brilliant book, *Tongues of Fire: The Explosion of Protestantism in Latin America*). The Protestant ethic may not be holding up in its original locales, in places like Sheffield; but it is thrivingly alive and well in Seoul, Soweto, and Santiago.

Neither movement supports secularization theory. The Muslim developments disclose the power of resistance to modernity in general, and secularity in particular, that contemporary people are capable of, even in contexts where modernization had gone quite far—as in the educated middle classes of the Middle East. The Evangelical movement shows that too, but it also shows that modernization can actually be spurred by explicitly religious values and behavior patterns. Now, it should be conceded that neither phenomenon nails secularization theory into a coffin for good. There are possible escape hatches. There is the "last gasp" spin on these events: Yes, the Iranian revolution is quite a spectacle, but sooner or later Iran will have to return to the modern world and then the secularizing forces will come back with a vengeance. As to the Evangelicals in places like Santiago, they may indeed repeat the history of their spiritual cousins in eighteenth- and nineteenth-century England: Their values and lifestyles may be helpful in an early stage of modern capitalist development; but if and when such development has been *successful*, the same values and lifestyles will cease to be helpful, and—so the argument goes—they will fade away, just as they did in England. At this moment in history it is not possible to state conclusively that these arguments are invalid; one can only say that they are speculative and that they go beyond the data now available.

A further difficulty for secularization theory is the religious character of the United States; since this country is of undeniable size and importance, the difficulty is considerable. No one will propose that the United States is not a modern society; indeed, in some respects it may be more modern than any other. Yet, by all conventional criteria, it continues to be an intensely religious country. By the same indicators, it is sharply different from Europe, and even from its immediate northern neighbor. (English-speaking Canada seems to be somewhere halfway between England and the United States, religiously speaking; Quebec has been undergoing a rapid and dramatic secularization process, much like Southern Europe, in the years since World War II.) Not only is the religious status quo maintained, but more Americans than ever regularly go to religious services, support religious organizations, and describe themselves as holding strong religious beliefs. To be sure, not all religious groups share in this bonanza. On the whole—again contrary to what secularization theory might predict—the churches prosper in direct relation to their adherence to received beliefs and practices: The more conservative, the more successful. Also, the United States contains a significant concentration of the aforementioned stratum of secularized educated people, a quasi-"Swedish" intelligentsia which, religiously speaking, has more affinity with Europe than its own society. As will be discussed later on, this cleavage between classes within American society has caused some sharp conflicts. Be this as it may, the massive fact of American religiosity, in what is certainly a highly modern society, and a very important one at that, creates a big difficulty for secularization theory. Neither the "last gasp" theory, nor the notion that religion will fade away with successful modernization, making its virtues obsolete, is very promising as an explanation of the American case.

I have long maintained that the situation of religion in the modern world needs an additional explanation which could perhaps be dignified by the phrase "pluralization theory." Briefly, this implies that pluralism is as important a fact as secularity in this context and that the latter becomes more comprehensible if one looks at both factors. By pluralism I mean more or less what the term means in ordinary usage—the co-existence with a measure of civic peace of different groups in one society. Religious pluralism (as distinguished from other kinds) is just one of several varieties of the phenomenon; pluralization is the process bringing about this condition. The term "co-existence" in the definition requires some amplification. In the present context it implies more than abstaining from mutual slaughter; rather, it denotes a certain degree of social interaction. This is important. There have been many situations throughout history in which different groups managed to exist side by side without indulging their probably congenital inclination to do each other in. Commonly, though, this desirable state of affairs (usually brought about not by lofty ideals of tolerance, but by the limits of either group's power) was maintained by the erection of barriers to social relations.

It is one of the more facetious illusions of liberal ideology that people will like each other better by getting to know each other. The opposite is the case, as a glance at the homicide data will show: Most murders are committed by close friends and relatives. The adage that good fences make good neighbors has a certain sociological validity. Example: The "fence of the law" erected by traditional Judaism around a Jewish people forced to live in a typically hostile Gentile environment. Another example: The Hindu caste system, allowing different groups (originally conquerors and conquered) to live side by side without having social relations. In most of these cases the two major tabus are against what anthropologists call commensality and connubium—taking meals together and marrying each other. The first, of course, has a way of leading to the second, and may be interpreted as subsuming most informal interaction. In such a situation there may indeed be civic peace, but the co-existence is very limited.

The pluralism that is of interest here occurs when the fences are breached. Neighbors lean over the fence, talk to each other, associate with each other. Inevitably, what then begins to occur I have termed "cognitive contamination"—the different lifestyles, values, and beliefs begin to mingle. This kind of pluralism has recurred periodically throughout history. Cities have often been a favorable locale for it. The great cities of the Hellenistic and late Roman period are an important case in Western history. What characterizes *modern* pluralism is its sheer massivity. Cities become gigantic and increasingly heterogeneous. More and more, people of wildly different cultures are forced to rub elbows all the time. But urbanization becomes a mental as well as a physical phenomenon. First through mass literacy, and then through modern mass communication, people encounter different cultures and worldviews without ever leaving their place of birth; in that sense, people can become urbanized in their outlook even if they live in places that the census classifies as small towns, villages, or rural areas. And since modernization is a continuing, progressive process, this pluralism too continues and deepens as time passes. Modernity in and of itself will do this. The pluralizing effects of modernity are further intensified by a market economy and a democratic polity. The market, like the city, has always been a pluralizing force: All sorts of people buy from and sell to each other, and as a result "commensality" is an ever-present possibility. Capitalism universalizes the market. Democracy, at least in its modern form, institutionalizes tolerance on the political level; again, there is the ever-present danger, from the viewpoint of closed traditional communities, that people who vote together may end up eating together—and after that *anything* can happen.

One thing that happens is, precisely, "cognitive contamination." It can be described quite simply: The thought obtrudes that one's traditional ways of looking at the world may not be the only plausible ones—that maybe these other people have a point or two. The worldview that until now was taken for granted is opened up, very slightly at first, to a glimmer of doubt. This opening has a way of expanding rapidly. The end point may then be a pervasive relativism. There are few certainties, convictions become mere opinions, and one becomes accustomed to considering just about any different view of things. One reason why America may be called the "lead society" (Talcott Parsons' expression) in terms of modern pluralism is that in America, for readily identifiable historical reasons, the process of pluralization has gone very far indeed. The language of American religion expresses this pluralistic dynamic very nicely: Americans have "religious preferences"; they "happen to be" this or that religious identity; they may even announce that they are "into" a particular religious adherence. The language proclaims uncertainty and impermanence: Preferences will probably change, one may decide that the happenstance of birth and upbringing need not be an inexorable fate, and one may be "into" a particular religious option today and out of it tomorrow.

If one understands this social and psychological dynamic, it will not be surprising that this kind of pluralism is likely to have secularizing effects. It would have these, I think, even in the absence of other secularizing factors, such as science and technology; it had such effects before, as in the Hellenistic period. Modernity can then be said to bring about an ongoing cross-fertilization of pluralism and secularity.

Another point should be made here: Modernity is a product of Western civilization, which in turn is a product of Hebrew religiosity and Greek reason. Both heritages make pluralism more difficult to cope with on the cognitive level. Hebrew religion insisted that there could be only one God, Greek reason that something could not be both A and non-A. The principle of monotheism and the principle of contradiction loom powerfully over the entire development of the Western mind. The contrast with southern and eastern Asia is very sharp. Almost any Indian or Chinese philosopher would regard both principles as patently absurd: One looks at reality and it becomes obvious that there are many, many manifestations of the divine; to reduce them to one single divinity is inherently implausible. And every sensible man knows, of course, that almost everything is *both A and* non-*A*. Thus Indian and Sinitic civilizations have been able to accommodate the "cognitive contaminations" of pluralism much more easily than the West, with its monotheistic and Aristotelian hang-ups. Hinduism is notorious for its capacity to absorb just about any god and any contradiction. Chinese and other East Asians are admirably agile in commuting between religious universes of discourse—they may be Confucians in their families, Buddhists during the great crises of life, and something else on other occasions. In this way, in addition to others not relevant here, Christianity is particularly vulnerable to the secularizing consequences of modern pluralism.

Christian communities that face the corrosive effects of pluralism have a limited number of options. For a while, of course they can ignore the whole matter and go on as if nothing had happened. The length of time during which this is possible will depend on the degree of "cognitive contamination" that is taking place. Once it can no longer be ignored, four basic options can be distinguished. Let me call them "cognitive bargaining," "cognitive surrender," and two subvarieties of "cognitive retrenchment," one defensive and one offensive. All can be observed in Christian churches today, in America and elsewhere.

It is possible to bargain with doubt. A kind of internal dialogue goes on within the believer, or within the community of believers. The dialogue can go something like this: "All right, there is no way of holding on to the miracles of Jesus. But we won't give up on the resurrection!" Or: "We'll stipulate that Jesus didn't say a number of things he's reported to have said in the

New Testament. But we'll insist that he instituted the Lord's supper!" Or: "We'll throw in the towel on papal infallibility. But we'll keep on maintaining the apostolic succession." And so on. It might be argued that some sort of bargaining process is inevitable once a body of beliefs meets a challenge that cannot be avoided. Liberal theology, at least since Friedrich Schleiermacher, has been one long episode of cognitive bargaining with the doubt engendered by modern secularity (its proponents, of course, being the "cultured despisers of religion" to whom Schleiermacher addressed himself). It might even be argued that this bargaining is the only honest course. However, it would be foolhardy to overlook its intrinsic dangers. One needs a very long spoon indeed if one is to dine with the devil of doubt; without it, one is liable to end up as dessert. Or, to vary the metaphor, the very first step in this bargaining process lands one on a slippery slope whose foot lies on the debris of shattered faith.

The other option is to avoid this painful process of give-and-take by hoisting a flag of surrender right away. This certainly simplifies matters, and it has been the modus operandi of many theologians claiming to be or described as radicals. In American Christianity a certain climax of this mode of theologizing was the so-called "death of God theology," a short-lived and media-promoted oxymoron. But many contemporary theologians using more moderate language are engaged in essentially the same act of surrender. The essence is the acknowledgement that modern secularity is correct in its denial of transcendence and the subsequent translation of the Christian message into this or that language of modern secularity. The language can be philosophical, psychological, or political: these different translations will have quite different consequences. But the basic assertion remains the same: *"This* is what Christian faith is *really* about." Not the embarrassing baggage of traditional orthodoxy, but whatever the secular substitute may be—the alleged "ethics of Jesus," some sort of existentialist experience, mental health with a "spiritual" component, or (the most popular version in recent years) some particular political agenda. While this modus operandi provides what one might call cognitive relief, in the end it is self-liquidating. Intellectually, it is a kind of suicide. Socially, it amasses concessions that end up being self-defeating, as people discover that one can be ethical without Jesus, existentially authentic and mentally healthy without religion, and most emphatically political without the church. This very process can be observed in stupefying detail in mainline American Protestantism today. A respectable number of Catholic theologians have been eager to follow the example, and one can even begin to observe the same syndrome among better-educated Evangelicals.

The contrary option is to defy the doubt and those who purvey it, to reaffirm the whole kit-and-caboodle of orthodoxy in the teeth of modern secularity, and whatever orthopraxy goes with it. In the defensive mode, this means to withdraw into a fortress within which all the old norms, doctrinal as well as behavioral, can be maintained. In the offensive mode the project is to reconquer society in the name of traditional religion. In other words, these are the options of the ghetto and of the crusade. Both options face formidable problems under modern conditions, especially in advanced industrial societies. The principal problem is, precisely, the pluralism under discussion here. If the ghetto option is followed—a more polite name would be creating or preserving a subculture—the walls around it must be very thick indeed if the cognitive contamination of pluralism is to be kept out. Allow one small chink in the wall, and the mighty wind of the surrounding pluralist culture is liable to come roaring in. Every sectarian community in American society has had to face this problem—from the Mormons and the Amish to the Hasidic Jews. But the most impressive case is that of Catholicism in the wake of the Second Vatican Council. Until then the Catholic church in America had successfully maintained a robust subculture whose inhabitants were kept relatively safe from the surrounding cognitive turbulence. Vatican II *intended*, in the words of John XXIII, to "open windows in the wall"; the unintended consequence of this so-called *aggiornamento* was to open an eight-lane superhighway through the center of the Catholic ghetto—*everything* came roaring in. The present leadership of the Catholic church, especially at Rome headquarters, is trying hard to repair the fortifications; chances are that it is too late, at least in Western countries.

Any attempt to reconquer society in the name of orthodoxy/orthopraxy, of course, implies an even more vehement rejection of pluralism. In the American context such a project necessitates not only a rejection of the constitutional separation of church and state, but also certain key portions of the American political creed. There are a few Catholic voices favoring such an improbable course, but the strongest proponents of this option can be found on the wilder shores of Evangelical Protestantism. The call here is for a "Christian America," narrowly defined in accordance with this particular version of orthodoxy. It requires no great sociological sophistication to see that such a project has little chance of success, barring presently unforeseen (and mercifully unlikely) national catastrophes. Most probably, every such crusade ends up in a little ghetto, with all the difficulties that entails. In the West the last promising effort in this direction was the Catholic-inspired Falangist revolution in Spain, with its avowed intention of reconquering Spain for "Christ the King" (a replication of the *reconquista* from Muslim domination). Intending to make Spain a suburb of Fatima, it only paved the way for what Spain is today—a suburb of Brussels.

However, just as it would be fallacious to see modernization and secularization as one-directional, irresistible processes, so would it be to see pluralization this way. There are strong impulses of counter-modernization and counter-secularization, and there are equally strong impulses of counter-pluralization. The reasons for the latter are easily stated: Pluralism creates a condition of permanent uncertainty as to what one should believe and how one should live; but the human mind abhors uncertainty, especially when it comes to the really important concerns of life. When relativism has reached a certain intensity, absolutism becomes very attractive again. Relativism liberates, but the resulting liberty can be quite painful; people then seek liberation from relativism. This is why strongly voiced projects promising certainty and "wholeness" have a large market in contemporary pluralist society, despite the aforementioned difficulties that any such absolutist project must face. Of course, not all these counter-pluralizing projects are religious in character. Many are political, or aesthetic, or linked with some distinctive lifestyle or philosophy. Thus, whatever their ideological differences, there are deep psychological and sociological affinities between Marxists, radical feminists, survivalists, practitioners of various health cults, and devotees of Ayn Rand. One is almost tempted to say that the ideological content of all such movements is of only marginal significance, *as long as* these movements can provide a renewed certainty of belief and behavior to those who embrace them.

To understand the social-psychological dynamics of pluralism is to understand the alternation between limitless tolerance and fanaticism that is so characteristic of contemporary Western, especially American culture, an alternation that would otherwise be very puzzling. On the one hand, this culture appears to tolerate nearly everything. No idea, no lifestyle, no agenda seems so far out that it will not be seriously discussed and conceded the right to exist. The very same people, though, who evince this pan-tolerance are peculiarly susceptible to conversion to some ideology claiming absolute certainty, demanding absolute loyalty, and making nonnegotiable demands on the rest of society. Relativists and fanatics not only live side by side today; they convert each other with predictable regularity.

It is not easy to live with pluralism. Democracy, both as an ideal and as a set of institutions, makes it easier in terms of practical, political arrangements, but it offers no help in coming to terms with the underlying existential problem. Taking a philosophical view of the matter, the challenge of modern pluralism to religion can be readily stated: It is a challenge to hold convictions without either dissolving them in utter relativity or encasing them in the false absolutes of fanaticism. It is a difficult challenge, but is not an impossible one.

2

Religion and Cultural Conflict in America Today

O ne need not be a social scientist to see that American society today is divided along a number of cultural fault lines. And being a social scientist is little if any help if one wants to make moral or theological judgments about these divisions. Social science can make only one, modest contribution to our understanding of this (or any other) situation, but it is a very useful contribution: Social science discloses the relationship between what people think and what they do—do not as individuals, for each human being is unique in some respects—but as members of groups and institutions.

What does it mean if one speaks of "cultural conflict" in America today? The term itself is not particularly difficult. The word "culture," in this context, has
the usual meaning given to it by social scientists—the
beliefs, values, and institutional arrangements by which
a group of people organize their lives, and where there
are contradictions and tensions in these configurations,
one can use the word "conflict." Now, it is important to
keep a sense of proportion, which is best achieved by
having a broad, cross-national perspective. Compared
to many other societies, the United States today has a
reasonably well-integrated culture; what is more, American culture continues to hold fascination for people all
over the world and it is unlikely to lose this status any-
time soon. Still, there *is* cultural conflict in America today, it is serious for those of us who live here, and it is
important to understand it.

Let us begin with a clear case, the current contro-
versy over abortion. Pitted against each other are two
groups of highly committed people whose assumptions
about reality and moral premises are diametrically opposed, and between whom civil dialogue has become
almost impossible. To put it starkly, one group believes
that an ovum six days after fertilization constitutes a
person entitled to the full protection of the law; the
other group believes that a fetus six months later has no
legal status other than being a part of a woman's body.
Given these totally different notions of what *is,* it
should not surprise us that the two groups draw totally
different moral conclusions as to what *ought* to be done.
As usual in political discourse, the banners under which
the battle is joined obfuscate the nature of the conflict.
"Pro-choice" is a meaningless phrase to those who believe that the "choice" here is one of homicide; "pro-
life" means nothing to those who see the issue as being

one of a woman's control over her own body, which, after all, is "life" too. Between the two groups of fully committed partisans, the conflict is as sharp as, say, between Christians and Muslims; indeed, it has an uncomfortably similar character of tribal ferocity. It is precisely the continuing integration of American society which prevents the conflict from taking on quasi-Lebanese dimensions, as does the simple fact that most Americans, by the evidence, are somewhere in the middle. The evidence of numerous opinion surveys can be read in different ways; I myself am inclined to think that most people are concerned about the issue, somewhat confused by it, and repelled by the strident rhetoric from both sides. Be this as it may, here is clearly a case where there is sharp conflict about beliefs and values between significant numbers of Americans.

The social scientist, in his professional capacity, is in no position to adjudicate the philosophical and theological issues underlying this conflict. He can certainly offer no guidance as to what ought to be done. What he can do, however, is to make some useful observations about the social context in which the conflicting parties are located. First, the social scientist can observe that views about abortion *do not stand by themselves*; rather, they tend to be *connected with other views*. Thus there are grounds for thinking that a strong "pro-choice" position on abortion is taken by people who, for example, are critical of the business community and reject the use of military force in American foreign policy. Conversely, people with a strong "pro-life" position are likely to be more sympathetic to business and to a vigorous defense posture. Very broadly speaking, "pro-choice" tends to be associated with left-of-center politics, "pro-life" with right-of-center. To be sure, these are probability statements; there are many exceptions. But if we are told that individual X has a strong "pro-choice" position, we can say that he or she probably favors heavy government interventions in the economy, is critical of American policy in Central America, and did not vote for Ronald Reagan; the fact that there are fervently right-wing Republicans who are staunch supporters of big business and are eager to use military force, who *also* favor abortion on demand, does not invalidate our probability statement. It is also well to remember that these particular correlations may change over time. Nevertheless, the important observation is that views about abortion, as with many other matters, come in *clusters*. Some individuals manage to tinker with these clusters in idiosyncratic ways; most people exhibit the clusters, if you will, as though ordered from central casting. This may be philosophically depressing, but it is *the* root fact of human life that modern social science has disclosed.

The next observation is equally important: These clusters of beliefs and values are *not randomly distributed throughout the population.* Let us make some more probability statements: Lower-income people of either gender are more likely to oppose abortion than upper-income people, again of either gender. Working-class people are more aggressive on foreign-policy issues than middle-class people. Professionals are more likely to be left-of-center politically than individuals of comparable income employed in business. And so on. Once more, of course, there are exceptions: We are making predictions based on statistically ascertained frequency distributions. And, once more, these distributions may change over time: Take, for instance, the political shift to the right, over several national elections, of blue-collar workers—and, conversely, the shift to the left of upper-income professionals. Leaving aside the details, what are we talking about now? We are talking about differences between people as a result of income, occupation, and education; in sociological terminology, we are talking about *class.*

There is a huge literature about class and class culture in America. For present purposes it is enough to say, with considerable assurance, that much if not all of the cultural conflict in present-day American society is related to class; put more precisely, most of the ideological clusters just mentioned are class-specific. The abortion issue is very clear in this: The major cleavages, by the evidence, are not due to gender, or to religion, but are very much dependent on class.

I can now turn to the gist of my sociological view of cultural conflict in today's America. This is, above all, a certain view of changes in the American class system (changes, by the way, which are very similar in all advanced capitalist societies, for instance in Western Europe; Japan, for reasons I cannot go into here, may possibly be the one important exception).

The basis of this view (sometimes called "New Class theory") are undisputed changes in the economy. The most important change, going back to the pre-World-War-II period in this country but greatly accelerating since the war, is the diminishing size of the labor force required to produce and maintain the material infrastructure of the society. Put simply, fewer and fewer people have been working in agriculture and mining, in manufacturing, and in the white-collar occupations directly associated with these processes of material production. The reason for this, of course, is the enormous and continuously increasing power of modern technology. This led first to a vast growth of all white-collar occupations, and then to a growth of those occupations that economists call the "quaternary sector"—better known as the service sector. That is still too broad a term for our purpose here. There is a subsector that provides services of a very distinctive kind—namely, non-material, knowledge-based services. The people employed in this sector make their living from the production and distribution of non-material knowledge. They consist of the huge army deployed in education at all levels, in those segments of public and private bureaucracy that deal with the administration of non-material goods—"human resources," "corporate image," "social justice," "quality of life," and the like—people in the media of mass communication, and (not necessarily least) people working in the therapy industry, from professors of psychiatry to geriatric sex counselors. All of these have a number of occupational characteristics in common, one of which is the somewhat elusive standard by which competence and performance are evaluated. The most important standard is the credentials obtained through an officially recognized educational process. Higher education of one sort or another, with college as a minimum, thus becomes the avenue by which one may enter this occupational world, and conversely the populating of this world has become a major function of the burgeoning system of higher education.

The central proposition of "New Class theory" is that these people in fact now constitute a new middle class, with important differences from the old middle class grounded in business and the older professions. There now exists a body of empirical data bearing on this proposition, and it seems reasonably tenable. The new knowledge professionals, holding income constant, differ significantly from the old middle class in their politics, their collective vested interests, and their culture—to make use of the term "class" defensible. Another way of describing the change is to say that the middle class has split in two: Where there was previously one middle class, stratified from upper-middle to lower-middle, there are now two middle classes, each with an internal stratification.

For example, both a professor of child psychology at an elite university who writes best-selling books on how to raise children and a poorly paid kindergarten teacher who applies the professor's ideas in actual practice belong to the new middle class. They do so despite the large difference in their income and status, by virtue of their common economic base and their shared class culture. It is also very likely that they themselves recognize that they belong to the same community.

As this new knowledge class grew in numbers and influence, it inevitably found itself in conflict with the old middle class from which it sprang—just as, a couple of hundred years ago in Europe, the rising middle class, or *bourgeoisie,* came into conflict with the aristocracy. The politics of the new knowledge class is to the left of the old middle class, and for reasons that are soundly based in its class interests: A much larger proportion of the knowledge class is directly employed or subsidized by government; it has, therefore, a vested interest in the expansion of those parts of government that provide it with employment and subsidization, and also with power and status. The knowledge class, therefore, favors the maintenance and expansion of the welfare state and government regulation of every conceivable kind. By contrast, the old middle class, or business class, regards these same expenditures as largely a burden, while it stands to gain from other government expenditures (notably defense spending and bailouts of failed business enterprises).

Take defense spending as an example: From the left this is often described as a choice of "guns or butter."

Fair enough: But one ought to ask, *whose* butter? The anti-war movement of the late 1960s created a slogan that can still be heard today—"reordering our national priorities." Its meaning is clear: National resources should be redirected from military to welfare projects. Sociologists are in the business of asking vulgar questions, and the vulgar question here must be, Who stands to gain from this reordering? The question answers itself. Now, in Western democracies the principal issue dividing right-of-center and left-of-center parties is precisely that of the nature, scope, and future course of the state as a provider of welfare and a regulator. It should come as no surprise, then, that the vested interests of the new knowledge class will pressure it toward the political left, while the interests of the business class press in the opposite direction. Needless to say, people in both groups convince themselves that their interests are also those of the nation as a whole or, in the case of the knowledge class, the interests of whatever underprivileged group is supposed to benefit from its services. Thus business people sincerely believe that what is good for business is good for America, and social workers believe with equal sincerity that what is good for them is good for the poor. Never mind for the moment how a disinterested observer might assess these philanthropic claims. My point here is, more simply, to shed light on the political preferences of these two groups of people.

But classes differ not only in their vested interests and their politics; they also differ in their culture. This is nothing new. Bourgeois culture, as it developed in Europe, did so in sharp distinction to the culture of the aristocracy. For example, the rising bourgeoisie revolutionized child-rearing. In sharp contrast with the aristocracy, bourgeois parents paid intense attention to their children, instituted a carefully thought-out regime of discipline and kindness, put greater emphasis on education, and, last but not least, looked upon childhood as a distinct and uniquely important phase in life. Today, the emerging culture of the knowledge class also differs significantly from the old middle-class culture. Some of these class differences have little if anything to do with the divergent class interests. Take dress codes as an obvious illustration. Business people typically wear three-piece suits and dress suits, while academics affect carefully scruffy outfits. It could just as well be the other way around. The only clear interest served by each code is to help members of the same class identify each other. But other aspects of class culture do have a direct relation to class interests. Very probably this is the case with abortion.

Why should upper-income women favor abortion, while lower-income women oppose it? Remember that while women are increasingly in the labor force, they are also in very different divisions of the labor force. This difference goes far toward explaining their divergent attitudes toward the family, motherhood, and children. Put in only slightly exaggerated form, children are a liability for an upwardly mobile professional, who derives much of her self-esteem from work and career; by contrast, children are one of the few assets in the lives of women who, if they work, work in jobs that provide little satisfaction and no status. Of course, the "liability" of children for upper-income professional women is only that in a limited sense—the sense of career—and most human beings, of any class, have other concerns than career and want children for emotional reasons unrelated to their vested interests. Let all of this be stipulated. Nevertheless, the existential differences between classes must still be taken into account when one tries to understand their differing positions on this issue.

Recent American politics makes much better sense

when one sees it in this perspective of class- and culture-struggle. The new class and its culture first came into view in the movements of the late 1960s and early 1970s. By the end of that period it had captured the national Democratic party as the principal political vehicle for its various causes. Conversely, the Republican party became the repository of groups for whom the ascendancy of the new knowledge class represented a threat. The so-called Reagan coalition was the result of this coming together of "resistance groups." Class politics makes strange bedfellows. The knowledge class must legitimate its interests by identifying with miscellaneous categories of putative victims in the lower reaches of society. The classical portrait of the resultant social comedy may be found in Tom Wolfe's account of Leonard Bernstein's party for the Black Panthers in the piece whose title coined the phrase "radical chic." The reaction of the old Republican elite—WASP denizens of board rooms, country clubs, and Episcopalian church parlors—to the new Reaganite constituency of enraged ethnics, blue-collar workers, and bucolic Evangelicals, all from places no one had ever heard from, still awaits a similar portrayal. Underneath the social comedy, however, are some pretty hard realities. One root reality is the clash between those whose major interest is in *production* and those with a major interest in *redistribution*; these commonalities of interest are strong enough for an English professor to feel an affinity with underclass juveniles and for a member of the Eastern Establishment to seek out alliances with people who think that Groton is a gum disease.

American religion, and particularly American Protestantism, have always had a special relationship to the class system. Some of the best-known writings in the sociology of religion—works by Max Weber, H. Richard

Niebuhr, Liston Pope, and others—have pointed out this relationship, which is peculiar to the United States and quite different from the social functioning of religion in other Western societies. Protestantism and its distinctive morality—which Weber called the "Protestant ethic"—were crucial in creating American middle-class culture; indeed, for a long time—certainly well into the last decade of the nineteenth century—that culture was Protestant to the core. Protestant church membership was one of the most important badges of middle-class status. Equally important, the different Protestant denominations served not only as class indicators but, especially for the lower classes, as agents of upward mobility. Thus, say in a New England town around the turn of this century, membership in the Episcopal or Unitarian churches indicated upper-class status, delicately set off from the middle-class constituency of Congregationalists and Presbyterians, and sharply separated from the *hoi polloi* who went to a Baptist or Methodist chapel or remained obstinately unchurched. Again and again, an individual from the lower classes who wanted to make his way up took the first step by joining one of the Protestant churches catering specially to his kind. In a very tangible way these churches served as "schools" for social mobility; they inculcated the bourgeois virtues without which social success was not possible. Thus, theologically speaking, an individual may now have been washed in the blood of the Lamb; speaking sociologically, in the same process he learned to wash his feet and also purge his speech of lower-class obscenities. American society has long been one of massive social mobility. As entire groups of people moved *en masse* into the middle class, their churches also attained respectability; at that point, other denominations took over their previous function as mobility training grounds. In this century, Pentecostal and Holiness churches have been the most important conduits for lower-class people into the "Protestant ethic" and thus into the promised land of bourgeois respectability.

This distinctively American symbiosis of religion and class has survived into our own time, especially in the lower reaches of the class system. It has been complicated by the increasing pluralization of American culture, especially the impressive social success of Roman Catholics and Jews, and further complicated by secularization in significant sectors of the middle class. I cannot pursue these changes here. But it is important to understand how religion relates to the aforementioned bifurcation of the middle class.

Take mainline Protestantism: Its constituency is overwhelmingly middle-class, with the majority belonging to the old business class rather than the new knowledge class; indeed, the latter probably represents the most secularized and unchurched segment of the population. The *clergy* of the same denominations, however, are a very different story: They, and the church bureaucracies and seminaries they staff, are very much part of the new knowledge class. They share in its culture, defer to its beliefs and values, and enthusiastically practice its politics. Understandably, there has been a widening gulf between clergy and laity in these denominations. For a while, some astute observers of the Protestant scene anticipated a great power struggle in the making. This struggle has not occurred. Disgruntled lay people didn't fight their clergy; rather, they quietly stole away. All of these denominations have had declining membership in recent years, some of them (Episcopalian in the lead) a catastrophic decline. There are several reasons for this, one important one being demographic: Upper-middle-class people have very few children. But it is clear that disillusionment on the part of many people in these churches has been a very important factor in the decline of membership. Throughout this time the membership of the Evangelical denominations has been growing quite rapidly. Some observers have concluded that this growth has been furthered by disgruntled mainline Protestants joining Evangelical churches. Recent research (I'm referring to the important book by Wade Clark Roof and William McKinney, *American Mainline Religion*) suggests that there is actually quite little emigration from the mainline to the Evangelical churches. The growth of the latter, as always, has come from two sources—higher fertility and recruitment from the masses below. As to the mainline churches, it appears they now serve as way stations for people heading out from *any* religious affiliation. Put sharply, these churches have now become *schools for secularity.*

The constituency of Evangelical Protestantism is very different. As with its historical antecedents, it is peopled by a much less prestigious (lower-middle and working-class), less educated, and more provincial membership. Not surprisingly, its role in the current cultural/class conflict has been very different. The clergy, the bureaucrats, and the official intellectuals of mainline Protestantism have been in the forefront of virtually all "New Class" crusades. Indeed, if an outside observer wanted a reliable and up-to-date compendium of the political agenda of the knowledge class, he would be well advised simply to follow the latest pronouncements of the National Council of Churches and of the mainline Protestant denominations. With rare omissions or modifications, these pronouncements faithfully reflect this political agenda. What the religious version does is to add a tone of righteous indignation and, of course, the claim that the same agenda represents God's will for our time. By contrast, Evangelicals have provided the troops for many of the political causes that might be described as "resistance movements" against the power-grab of the knowledge class, especially in the area of family and sexuality—but also in foreign, defense, and economic policy. This is not to say that all Evangelicals are politically right-of-center; the data show that they are not. But Evangelical Protestantism has supplied potent symbols, leadership, and committed activists for many right-wing causes. And, in contrast to the mainline, there is much less of a rift here between leadership and laity. In some denominations in this community of discourse, notably in the Southern Baptist Convention, the leadership has actually been grabbed by the most staunchly reactionary group. It is not clear whether this will last. As James Hunter has shown, education is likely to do these groups in, as it arguably did to their upper-class cousins: As Evangelical seminaries and colleges seek accreditation and acceptance in the wider society, they will inevitably come to accept the beliefs and values of the new middle-class culture. This has already happened in the so-called Evangelical Left, a beachhead of "New Class" culture on the rougher shore of American Protestantism. It is not very difficult to imagine the situation a few years from now, say in the later part of the first decade of the next century. By then the membership of the mainline churches will have been further decimated. There will be few Episcopalian clergy left to man the barricades. But by then other groups, such as the Southern Baptists, will probably have moved into the mainstream and in the process will have acquired the latter's class culture. It will then be clergy from these newly assimilated denominations who will celebrate whatever causes will be politically correct in this social milieu by then.

I cannot here discuss how these changes have affected the non-Protestant communities. The situation in Judaism is obviously complicated by the factor of ethnicity, which introduces a distinctive dynamic of its own. The same is still true of Christian Eastern Orthodoxy. The Roman Catholic community, however, has been buffeted by very much the same forces just discussed. There has been a similar fault line between clergy and laity, and a power-grab by "New Class" staffs within the ecclesiastical bureaucracy and communications media; the result is that (with one or two exceptions, notably with regard to abortion) the statements of the American Catholic bishops in recent years would serve an outside observer almost as well as the pronouncements of mainline Protestantism in his efforts to understand the agenda of the knowledge class. However, the authoritarian and international structure of Roman Catholicism serves as a brake on this development: The laity has nowhere else to go unless it wants to abandon the faith, something that even the most progressive Catholics are unwilling to do. And the bishops, however much they may want to be accepted by the elite culture, have crusty old Rome looking over their shoulders.

Where is this process of cultural conflict and class dynamics likely to go? I have learned to be cautious in making sociological predictions. But I do not see American society as being in a dangerous crisis and, barring a catastrophe, I do not see it moving toward such a crisis in the foreseeable future. Nor do I see either side in this cultural conflict achieving a clear-cut victory. Each side will win some and lose some. There will also be compromises in several areas, including (I think) the difficult one of abortion. If I were to risk one general prediction, it would be this: Take as a baseline what the "New Class" stood for when it first thundered onto the public scene some twenty years ago. I would predict that most of the political and economic planks of the earlier platform will be thrown off: There will be no "revolution," either politically or economically; the United States will continue to be, essentially, the same democratic-capitalist society it is today, and where necessary it will defend its interests militarily. I venture this prediction because very few societies in history have voluntarily destroyed themselves—as the "revolutionary," socialist, and pacifist programs of the late sixties would have done. On the other hand, I would also predict that most of the so-called "social issues" of that early platform will win out, especially those concerning gender, sexual behavior, child-rearing, and the ethos of personal relationships in general. *This* prediction is based on the assumption that very few people voluntarily give up behavior that they have found to be pleasant and convenient. These predictions give a picture, not of crisis, but of compromise. Whether one considers such an outcome good or bad will depend on one's values. In terms of mine, this outcome would be a mixed bag, with the good outweighing the bad. If the kind of revolution being proclaimed in the late sixties had really taken place, this would have meant the destruction of democratic capitalism in the West and thus the best hope for a decent future not only in the West but in much of the world. This is a very great good. Also, there are some positive aspects in the ideology at issue here, first among them the sharp decline of racial intolerance. But there is also a deeply ingrained tendency toward utopian fantasies (these do not have to be on the Left), an unattractive preoccupation with self, and a general disposition to whine. A mixed bag, to be sure—but history hardly ever offers us a better deal.

3

The West and the Challenge
of Cultural Pluralism

At a gathering devoted to issues of American foreign policy, shortly before the final collapse of the Soviet Union, one of the participants asked a pithy question: "We have won. Why doesn't it feel like it?" The question, I think, reflects a widespread mood of self-doubt, especially in culturally elite milieus, not only in the United States but in Western Europe as well. The current debate over "multiculturalism" reflects the same mood, at least among some of the participants and interestingly on both sides of the issue. Those in favor of multicultural programs in education very frequently evince a deep dislike of Western civilization, allegedly characterized by racism, sexism, violence, contempt for the environment, and other vices. For them, we must look to other cultures for more humane values. But those on the other side, who insist on the traditional emphasis on Western civilization and Western values, frequently seem to have very little confidence in the capacity of the West to prevail in any kind of cultural contestation. Thus even the introduction of a modest amount of non-Western materials into the school curriculum is perceived as a serious threat to the integrity of the culture. There is here a sense of decline, a failure of nerve, that might with some precision be described as decadent. Yet it should be stressed that this is, in the main, an elite phenomenon. It is most common in the most educated, most privileged sectors of Western societies. The rest of the population continues to be chauvinistically self-satisfied, either oblivious of or angered by what is said in the higher circles. Here are the not-so-silent majorities whose militantly nationalistic sentiments are ready to break out if given a proper opportunity, the constituencies for xenophobia, protectionism, and saber rattling.

It is not the first time in history that a cultural elite has stood in the forefront of those who would give up on their society. Yet in the contemporary situation of Western societies there are contradictory movements even within the cultural elite, especially in the United States: to wit, a cultural imperialism, quite unconscious of itself, which co-exists in a strange symbiosis with the aforementioned decadence. The same people who are prepared to admit that their culture is no better and quite possibly worse than any other, will make moral judgments and advocate actions that presuppose the absolute validity, indeed superiority, of Western institutions and ideas. One can observe this in the way that people in places like Harvard or Stanford take for granted that Western-style democracy is the infallible moral measure of political regimes throughout the world, or that Western-style ideas about human rights (including the feminist version) can be exported to every country on earth. If Western elite culture is decadent, then its decadence has some interesting complexities.

Decadence has always had a masochistic component. In culture as in sex, the masochist confronts a real or imagined conqueror, whose robust aggression is admired and deliciously submitted to. Ever since Tacitus invented the noble Germans to serve as a counter-image to his own, putatively decadent Rome, there have been recurring fantasies of physically and morally superior people against whom one's own society has neither the strength nor the right to prevail. In modern literature one of the sharpest portraits of this attitude is Constantine Cavafy's poem "Waiting for the Barbarians," in which he depicts the upper crust of Roman society eagerly expecting ravishment by the approaching savage hordes. The self-denigrators of contemporary Western societies have gone through a number of such masochistic fantasies. In the 1930s they were directed toward the fascist regimes in Europe which at that time, it is salutary to remember, appeared to many to represent a superior and historically inevitable movement. Among intellectuals it was the Soviet Union and other socialist regimes or movements that for a long time represented this irresistible force that would rightfully vanquish their own society. I am not at all sure that the events of the last few years have laid this particular fantasy to rest for good; the utopian imagination has an immense capacity to ignore or reinterpret empirical evidence. But one continuing version of masochistic self-denigration is what, first in France, has been called "Third World-ism"—the belief that non-Western cultures are health-ier, happier, more humane than the West, and that the future belongs and should belong to them. It is this be-lief, of course, that constitutes an important theme in the propaganda of multiculturalism. It is too early to say whether Japan and perhaps the other successful societ-ies of East Asia may become yet another embodiment of the admired conqueror. At the time of writing there is more fear than admiration in the Western reaction. Psychologically there is only a short step from Japan-bashing to Japanophilia.

What is one to make of all this? I think that it is possible to avoid self-denigration without falling into the opposite stance of self-satisfied chauvinism. As I will argue later on, religious faith is one powerful help in maintaining a reasonable distance from the ever-changing intellectual fashions of elite culture. But there are also some simple facts to hold onto as one considers the position of Western culture in the contemporary world.

The one overriding fact to consider—a fact that has become one of the truisms of the age, but which is true nonetheless—is that of cultural pluralism. The situation can be easily described: Through most of history, most human beings found themselves in a lifelong, single, highly integrated cultural environment; by contrast, to-day most human beings in the world—and the great majority in advanced industrial societies—constantly encounter foreign cultures, either by actual contact with representatives of those cultures or through various in-formation media. The basic causes of this are also easily discerned, especially scientifically based technology, which has created an industrial economy, as well as the means of rapid transport and instantaneous communication that increasingly unify the globe. These powerful forces are at work worldwide, although obviously they are most powerful in the societies with the highest technological sophistication. The United States has the additional feature of being the only very large industrial society (there are some less populous ones, like Canada and Australia) that has historically been open to mass immigration. Not only that, the United States—in sharp contrast to Western Europe and Japan—is legally, socially, and culturally geared to receiving and absorbing large numbers of immigrants from every conceivable country.

But pluralism is not just a lot of people of different colors, languages, religions, and lifestyles bumping into each other and somehow coming to terms under conditions of civic peace. It is not merely a fact of the external social environment. Pluralism also impinges on human consciousness, on what takes place within our minds. This internal, subjective process is what I have called "pluralization." Cultural plurality is experienced by the individual, not just as something external—all those people he bumps into—but as an internal reality, a set of options present in his mind. In other words, the different cultures he encounters in his social environment are transformed into alternative scenarios, options, for his own life. The very phrase "religious preference" (another American contribution to the language of modernity!) perfectly catches this fact: The individual's religion is not something irrevocably given, a *datum* that he can change no more than he can change his genetic inheritance; rather, religion becomes choice, a product of the individual's ongoing project of world- and self-construction. There is a very revealing phrase of American idiom: "I don't yet know what I'll be when I grow up." This phrase is uttered, not just by daydreaming teenagers, but by people in their thirties or forties. It is said in a half-joking tone, but it reflects a serious reality—that of people who make fundamental self-defining choices long into adult life. When it comes to religion it might, for example, cross the lips of a fifty-year-old who has just been converted to Buddhism, but who wonders whether this will be his last conversion or just another stage in a series of personal transformations. Put simply, on the level of human consciousness modernization is a movement from fate to choice, from a world of iron necessity to one of dizzying possibilities. This change can be truthfully described as a great liberation. But one must also understand the discontents and even terrors that can come with this new freedom.

I have argued above that pluralization brings with it a relativization of all normative contents of consciousness. As long as the individual has before him only one cohesive set of cultural norms, these norms take on in his own mind the quality of inevitability: This is what the world is, and it could be no other; this is who I am, and I could be no other; and here is how I ought to live. Put differently (in the words of Alfred Schutz), the individual lives in a world taken for granted that leaves very few options open. But all of this changes when different cultural blueprints become available (Schutz would say, they come to be "at hand" and, therefore, possible). Clearly, the person who is blessed with all these choices has a greater measure of freedom; by the same token, however, he has lost his old capacity for certitude. Beliefs and values that once inhibited the zone of basic certainties now move to a more volatile zone of opinions, tentative preferences, *ad hoc* and therefore reversible decisions. Again using Schutzian language, beliefs and values are now held "until further notice."

This situation is uncomfortable, to say the least. We may experience a great sense of exhilaration upon being liberated from the taken-for-granted structures of a traditional culture, and in all likelihood there are some individuals who can keep up such an exhilarated attitude throughout life. But most people want *some* certainties, *some* beliefs and values that can be more or less taken for granted. This is particularly so in the cases of religion and morality, the twin foundations of most people's meaningful cosmos. There arises, therefore, a frequently desperate longing for certainties, and this in turn leads many individuals to sudden conversions to some absolutist cognitive and normative system. To understand the social psychology of this is to understand the otherwise strange alternation between total tolerance and total intolerance that is so common in modern (and modernizing) societies. It is also, alas, to undermine the liberal belief that cultural pluralism must necessarily lead to greater tolerance of diversity: It will probably do so—for a while. But when the burden of relativity becomes too heavy, this tolerance may suddenly collapse, and a raving dervish may explode into what until then was an amicable seminar of intercultural communication. The children of upright, thoroughly Protestant, Middle American types become liberated bohemians who will tolerate everything except intolerance; "So you are a cannibal? How interesting! I think that we would all benefit greatly if we understood your point of view more fully." *Their* children are prone to become converts to whatever religious, political, or aesthetic fanaticism happens to cross their path. And what can happen to individuals can also happen to much larger groups, indeed entire societies.

This analysis apparently presents us with an unattractive choice, broadly speaking, between cultural wimps and cultural thugs. Is there really no other option?

Personally, I do not find it particularly difficult to take an equidistant position between a blindly ethnocentric triumphalism and the masochistic attitude that is infinitely tolerant of every culture except one's own. The present age provides unprecedented opportunities to understand and learn from other cultures: I would contend that to be a civilized person today includes the capacity to take advantage of these opportunities. It is inevitable that in such a process of intercultural contact *both* parties to the transaction will change, be the parties individuals, groups, or entire societies. Thus it is not only likely but in many ways desirable that Western culture will undergo changes as a result of the current wave of pluralization. The lively debate over the applicability of Japanese management practices in America is a good example: The emerging consensus holds that there is much to be learned from the Japanese in this area, that some of their methods can be easily applied in this country and others not, and finally (most important) that many Americans may not *want* to adopt some aspects of Japanese economic culture—not because this cannot be done, but because to do so would go against our deeply held beliefs in the sovereignty of the individual and in his right to privacy.

If one believes in the humanity of others, then one must take seriously the possibility that their experience has something to teach, and perhaps deserves to be emulated. But if one has any beliefs or values at all, and recognizes that these are grounded in one's culture, then the conclusion of deeming one's own culture superior at least to those that deny the validity of these beliefs and values cannot be avoided. If I believe that cannibalism is wrong, then *ipso facto* I believe that my non-cannibalistic culture is superior to all those where people eat each other—at least in this respect. Conversely, the totally tolerant individual is *ipso facto* an individual who holds nothing to be true, and in the final analysis perhaps an individual who *is* nothing. And that is the soil that grows fanatics.

There is a story told by James Morris in his wonderful history of the British Empire about Charles Napier, who among other exploits conquered the Sind in 1843 and installed there the usual minimalistic order of British rule. One of its great impositions was the prohibition of *suttee*: The British tolerated any number of native eccentricities, but they were not willing to tolerate the burning of widows. The Brahmans of Sind defended *suttee* as an age-old custom. Napier's retort was splendidly simple: "My nation also has a custom. When men burn women alive, we hang them. Let us all act according to national custom!" I am not suggesting that we should return to the undoubtedly arrogant (and not a little racist) sense of cultural superiority that animated many Victorian imperialists. To that extent, twentieth-century cultural pluralism has (or should have) made us humbler. There are many aspects of Hindu civilization before which we ought to stand in awe; there are almost certainly aspects in which it is superior to the West (such as its much deeper sense of the vastness of time). But General Napier's moral revulsion against *suttee* expresses a fundamental Western value, that of the inviolability and unique worth of every human individual, which we can confidently assert as superior to the values that underlie widow-burning. The same attitude of balanced humility and self-affirmation can apply to the whole gamut of Western ideas and institutions.

If one believes in the rights of the individual, then one must believe in the superiority of the Western legal system that has uniquely institutionalized these rights. If one holds a moral preference for people having enough to eat as against people starving, then one must deem Western-derived capitalism a superior way of arranging the economy. None of these positions preclude criticisms of one's own society and of its institutions any more than they preclude respect for other cultures; but they presuppose that one's own experience has yielded some measure of truth. This is why the charge of "cultural imperialism" if often facile: Any affirmation of truth is "imperialistic" since it must presuppose its superiority over the corresponding affirmation of error.

The relative ease with which one can, in principle, take such an intermediate position on the issue of cultural pluralism does not necessarily mean that such a position is likely to win out. Both dogmatism and nihilism can be theoretically liquidated; unfortunately, there are battalions of flesh-and-blood dogmatists and nihilists who remain happily unaware of this fact. Thus one cannot easily dismiss the possibility that the present pan-tolerance may suddenly transmute into frenetic intolerance. Such a malignant mutation could be triggered by any number of events, the likeliest being a prolonged economic crisis. Both in North America and in Western Europe some such effects can already be observed—resentful nationalism, protectionism fueled by paranoia (especially with regard to Japan), xenophobia (especially against immigrants and *Gastarbeiter*), and intermittent explosions of virulent racism. It is all the more important to understand the profound psychological nexus between this type of fanaticism and the nihilism that is the consequence of total relativization.

Most of what has been said here about Western culture applies, *mutatis mutandis*, to the Western church. Obviously one aspect that is *mutandum* is the church's claim to universality, a claim that has always been made theologically, but which is now increasingly becoming an empirical fact. The demographic change in world Christendom has been repeatedly noted and it is not necessary to belabor it here. The simple fact is that the majority of Christians are now outside the boundaries of Europe and North America; that is, Christians are increasingly inhabitants of the Third World. In the case of the Roman Catholic church, the demographic center is now in Latin America, with Africa quickly moving up. Evangelical Protestantism is exploding all over Latin America, in black Africa, and in most of eastern Asia. There is an old Cuban folksong in which God is asked not to forget the *angelitos negros*, the little black angels. Such reminders are hardly required today. Even so sedate and originally culture-specific an institution as the Anglican church is well on the way to being de-Europeanized, as can be visually ascertained by looking at the group photographs or films of successive Lambeth conferences.

These demographic transformations in the Christian constituency have engendered considerable social and cultural tensions. No longer can the major Christian denominations be considered religious extensions of Western civilization, let alone agents of Western imperialism. And there are many practical problems of cultural adaptation, perhaps sharpest now in sub-Saharan Africa where such issues as polygamy and exorcism preoccupy the church authorities. Missiologists have used the term "enculturation" to refer to the process of social and cultural adaptation undergone by originally Western churches as they become established in non-Western environments. The most vexing question here, of course, is where to draw the line between adaptations that are theologically legitimate (no matter how practically or psychologically difficult they may be) and other adaptations that, if made, would violate essential tenets of Christian faith or morality. Different Christian traditions will necessarily vary in how they deal with this problem. But however the boundaries are drawn, the fundamental problem remains that two millennia of history cannot be undone. Christianity and Western culture have interacted symbiotically for so many centuries that they are now exceedingly difficult to disentangle. This means that, however one may emphasize the theological and empirical universality of the Church, there are aspects of its very faith—as well as of its institutional structure—that make its clearly Western provenance obvious. Therefore, non-Westerners who participate in the life of the Church (even the most "enculturated" one) must also participate in experiences of an indelibly Western character. One of the core values of any Christian morality is the irreplaceable worth of the human individual, from which flows the entire modern conception of human rights. Yet this core value is inseparable from the whole course of Western civilization and of Western civilization *only*. The Chinese Christian who affirms this particular value is willy-nilly affirming with it an innate superiority of Western civilization over the communalistic and hierarchical cultures of Asia. It would be a matter of helpful honesty if this point were conceded by the more enthusiastic "enculturators."

Needless to say, there is an additional dimension to the Church's confrontation with cultural pluralism which derives from the fact that it claims to be much more than just a social institution or a repository of cultural values and a source of moral insights. The Church claims to possess ultimate truths that are available nowhere else. The confrontation with other cultures, therefore, inevitably means an encounter with competing claims to ultimate truth.

Different branches of the Church have responded to this encounter in different ways. There continues to be the old missionary stance, which simply relegates the competing truth claims to the category of error and seeks to convert the erring. This is the religious version of old Western ethnocentrism. It is characteristic of the Evangelical community, of the more conservative elements in Roman Catholicism, and of scattered remnants of orthodoxy or neo-orthodoxy in the mainline Protestant denominations. There is also the religious version of the aforementioned cultural masochism, which is particularly widespread among liberal Protestants, which denigrates just about everything within the Western religious tradition, all the way back to its Israelite and Hellenic roots, in an invidious comparison with this or that non-Western worldview. Prominent among these cultural self-despisers are theologizing feminists, who regard the Western tradition as an oppressive patriarchate, and environmentalists, who characterize the Judeo-Christian religion as a great alienation from nature. It hardly matters that the non-Western counter-images to these alleged Christian pathologies are to some extent imaginary; these putative non-Western and non-Christian approaches to the world are only held up in order to denigrate the culture and religious heritage of the West.

Once again, we have an unattractive choice between thugs and wimps, this time theological ones. And once again, I would contend, there is the possibility of a *via media* that avoids the Rambos on one side and the Mary Poppinses on the other. One way of adumbrating this possibility is to clarify what one may mean by the phrase "inter-religious dialogue."

If by dialogue one means that representatives or adherents of different religious traditions talk to each other about their differences, then this is not so much a matter of choice as of necessity: It can only be avoided, under modern conditions, if one takes shelter in a carefully maintained or reconstructed sectarian ghetto. This is indeed an option, though it is costly and not very promising over the long run. Dialogue can also mean a polemical engagement (*Streitgespräch*) with other religious traditions, with the purpose of showing up the latter's errors and converting one's interlocutors. This is the sort of one-sided encounter that Christian authorities used to inflict on the Jews under their jurisdiction. Among other things it has had the effect of implanting such deep revulsion in Jewish minds that even now many Jews suspect this is what Christians have in mind when they speak of dialogue. And then there are two other types of dialogue going on today that are unobjectionable in themselves, and in some situations very worthwhile, but finally not interesting religiously. These could be called the anti-defamation and the coalition dialogues. One is intended to reduce prejudice and negative stereotypes by providing accurate information about one's own tradition. Clearly one could not possibly object to this in situations where adherents of any religious tradition are defamed or discriminated against. The other sort is dialogue with a very pragmatic goal, namely to discover commonalities in order to form coalitions for this or that secular purpose. In principle, this could be for any purpose at all—to feed the hungry, to propose (or oppose) social legislation, to resist (or support) a war or revolution, and so on. Whether or not one finds such dialogue worthwhile will, of course, depend on one's feelings about the project at issue.

Finally there is the sort of dialogue that might better be called "contestation"—a serious, no-holds-barred confrontation between competing truth claims *on the level of truth*. To enter such a dialogue is dangerous unless one has a very clear and confident idea of one's own experiences of truth. If one lacks such an idea, one will in short order be sucked into the worldview of whoever *does* have clarity and confidence. Therefore: No wimps! On the other hand, one cannot enter such a dialogue *honestly* (that is, without a covert missionary or pragmatically exploitative agenda) without accepting the risk that one's own position might change as a result of this encounter. Therefore: No thugs! Such dialogue becomes a common journey toward truth. The Christian embarking on such a journey will naturally believe that no future destination can invalidate what he now holds to be the truth; if he thought otherwise, he could hardly be called a Christian. He must, however, accept in principle the possibility that *another* truth might supersede his own, or that (more likely) his conception of the truth will have to be modified at various points. Dialogue entered upon with such presuppositions will be existentially risky, intellectually unpredictable, and sometimes socially awkward if not rude. It also holds the promise of new intuitions and insights.

It is largely because of my conviction that such a contestation between the faith held by the Church and other faiths is actually possible and potentially fruitful that I am not finally troubled by the impact of cultural pluralism. The pluralizing forces of modernity do indeed relativize all belief systems, but the truth will come out again and again. *Truth resists relativization*. To that extent one might say that the forces of modernity, over time, separate the wheat from the chaff. This puts the Church into a situation that is surprisingly similar to the one in which it started out—the late Roman Empire, with its bewildering plurality of religions, cultures, moralities, and what nowadays are called lifestyles. All the great cities of the modern world evoke Alexandria. It is not extravagant to hope that the explosive pluralism of our time may again bring forth new theological syntheses. These observations, though, take us from the social and cultural contexts of faith to consideration of this faith itself.

Part II

—∽—

Believers and Belief

4

The Solitary Believer

Those of us who worship in liturgical churches regularly join in reciting the Nicene Creed, which begins with the lapidary affirmation, "I believe in one God." Much of the time, of course, this sentence is uttered without reflection. This does not necessarily mean that it is uttered insincerely—most of what we say, even a deeply felt sentence like "I love you," is said without reflection. But if we step back and begin to turn the Nicene affirmation around in our minds, at least three problems present themselves: Who is the "I" that is affirming faith? What does "believe" mean in this context? And who is the "one God" in whom belief is being affirmed? Each of these questions is awesomely vast in its implications, and I am neither megalomaniac nor humorless enough (the two are actually one) to pretend that I have definitive answers. What I will do in the following pages is turn the questions round and round. I will, to be precise, reflect about them. In the course of this reflection I will indeed make some affirmations, but—as becomes anyone with a sense of humor—I will not make them in a tone of ringing certitude.

It happens that the movement of so-called liturgical reform has introduced a different formulation of this and the other historic creeds: Instead of saying "*I* believe" the congregation is now supposed to say "*we* believe." The purpose of this change is to emphasize the communal character of Christian faith. It also implies a currently fashionable critique of the alleged aberration of modern Western individualism; it further implies that the Christian community is to rescue the modern individual from a state of solitary alienation. But for the moment leave aside any scrutiny of either the biblical or the sociological assumptions undergirding this rationale, and simply ruminate on the differences in meaning between the two.

To say "I believe" is to set myself off as an individual against other individuals who do not. It is a statement that commits myself. In the classical sense, it is a *confessional* statement. In Christian history, confession was very often the prelude to martyrdom: I confess a belief for which, if need be, I am prepared to suffer and die. The statement "we believe," at least in contemporary speech, has an altogether different connotation. It describes a particular collectivity that is set off against other collectivities. I—to use a very common American phrase—"happen to" belong to this collectivity rather than any of the others, perhaps by personal choice, but more likely because of the accident of birth. This is not a confessional statement that commits me. It is rather— to use another highly revealing American phrase—a statement of "religious preference." It belongs to the language of consumer behavior, not to the language of martyrdom.

The "we" in this reformulation is a deliberate *avoidance* of the "I." A lot is avoided by this—the solitariness (if you will, the alienation) of this "I"—but equally so its accountability, its status as a responsible actor. This "we" is descriptive in a non-commital way, as when one says "we Americans prefer baseball to soccer," or "we Europeans keep the knife in our right hand while we use the fork with our left." It is that "we" which Martin Heidegger designated by the untranslatable German phrase *"das Man"* (as in the idea of "one" in English— "one does not eat spinach with one's knife"—this "one," which at the same time is everybody, and nobody). Heidegger called existence in *das Man* "inauthentic," a view that presupposes the solitary "I" as truly authentic. José Ortega y Gasset had the same idea with his concept of *"lo que se hace"*—"that which one does"— the principle of living a conventional life in society, following its rules not only in behavior but in thought. Ortega, like Heidegger, deplored this mode of existence.

Which formulation of the Nicene Creed do I want to use? The decision reaches far beyond the liturgical context. It is a decision between two views of the true self: Is it the self that stands alone in the face of reality, apart from and perhaps even against its community? Or is it the self securely embedded in community, specifically the one in which its biography is rooted? Beyond this weighty question there is another, equally weighty: If the solitary individual can be understood as the result of a distinctive Western history, should this history be viewed as a great achievement or a great aberration?

Let it be stipulated that human beings have always possessed a self, ever since *homo sapiens* emerged from a moment in evolution about which (perhaps mercifully) we know relatively little. But even if we stipulate such an anthropologically constant self, it is very clear that in the course of history this self was both experienced and reflected upon in very different ways. In any part of the world, if one goes far enough back in time one comes upon a mode of experience and thought that I would call the mythological matrix. Its features are by now well understood and have been particularly well treated in the work of Eric Voegelin and Mircea Eliade. In this mythological world the boundaries between self and non-self are fluid: The individual self is embedded in a continuity of being that extends from the human community through what we today call "nature" to the realm of the gods or other sacred entities. The self in this world is definitely, emphatically, not solitary. There are good reasons to think that the consciousness of every young child starts out by replicating key features of this mythological matrix. If so, it would be very imprudent ever to assume that the mythological world view is finished with; it would also help explain the nostalgia that even very modern people seem to have for this world in which everything, in the fullest sense of the word, was "whole."

As particularly Voegelin has shown, this mythological worldview was ruptured at different times and in different parts of the world. With each rupture (although Voegelin does not use this term) a certain individuation occurred—the individual was taken out of the unbroken continuity between community, cosmos, and gods. It would be a mistake to look upon this break with the fully embedded self as (for better or for worse) an exclusively Western phenomenon. It certainly occurred in at least two other civilizations: in India, where the individual in quest of release or enlightenment breaks out of the communal bonds, especially those of caste; and, in a very different way, in China, where the process of self-cultivation—especially in its Neo-Confucian version—also resulted in a kind of "individualism." And there may have been other non-Western cases of what Voegelin calls "leaps in being." In the West the rupture has two clear sources: in ancient Israel, where the individual emerged from the confrontation with God, and in ancient Greece, where a different individuation took place by means of reason. The history of the Western self is rooted in the merging of these two streams of individuating experience and thought, represented by Jerusalem and Athens. It is not misleading to use the term "Western individualism" to describe the product of this historical process.

It is also quite clear, however, that modernity has ushered in yet another phase of this history. It has accentuated the individuation characteristic of earlier periods of Western history; if you will, the self has become yet more solitary. At the same time, and perhaps because of this, it has brought forth strong impulses toward de-individuation, toward a repudiation of some or all of "Western individualism." These movements of history are reflected in the development of Western thought. The development might be said to have begun in earnest when Descartes, in his elegant statement *"cogito ergo sum,"* proposed the knowing subject as the only firm foundation of our knowledge of reality. The demise of this philosophical individualism was announced early in this century by Ernst Mach's proposition that, because of the insights of modern science, the self can no longer be salvaged (*"das unrettbare Ich"*). The currently fashionable schools of post-modernistic or deconstructionist theory are but other variations on this theme of de-individuation. These developments in the history of ideas can probably be studied by themselves. But it is important to remember, not only that theorists are a small minority but that they live in society like everyone else and have lives and relationships that make their theories plausible to themselves as well as others. Put simply, in the life of even the most abstruse philosopher, experience precedes reflection. The dynamics of individuation and de-individuation in the modern world, therefore, cannot be understood only as an episode in the history of ideas. One must consider the social situation in which experiences take place that provide plausibility for one set of theories as against another. I have long argued that *pluralism* is a crucially important feature of the modern situation.

Pluralism denotes a state of affairs in which no single group constitutes the society as a whole and, in consequence, no group can serve as an all-embracing community for its members. This has enormous implications for the individual and his beliefs. Neither the individual's self nor his worldview can any longer be taken for granted. Inexorably, the self is forced into solitariness and any worldview becomes a matter of deliberate choice. Modernity is not the only age that has produced such pluralistic situations, but it has made pluralism a uniquely massive and increasingly global reality. "Urbanity" neatly describes the human type emerging from the pluralistic situation—emancipated from the parochial solidarity of his original community (if you will, alienated from his roots) and from any body of taken-for-granted beliefs. This is a human type characterized by a high degree of *freedom*, defined as a state in which the individual can make many choices.

I will now make another simple but far-reaching point: *Only an individual with such a degree of freedom can be said to "believe" at all.* And again: *Freedom presupposes solitariness. Thus it is only the solitary individual who can engage in an act of believing.*

Imagine an individual who is far removed from urbanity, whether modern or pre-modern, who is securely embedded in a strong, all-embracing community. This individual, as we have stipulated anthropologically, has a self. But this self is never detached from his community: His identity is determined by his membership of the community. To use social-scientific language, there is very high symmetry (it can never be quite total) between objective and subjective identity. Such an individual is certainly not solitary, not alienated. But neither can he be said to be free, at least not in any empirically available sense. His life and his relation to reality are a matter of destiny, not choice. So is his relation to the gods of his community. Can such an individual be said *to believe* in these gods? Hardly. The gods here are part and parcel of taken-for-granted reality. Their existence and specific traits are assumed, indeed "known." No act of faith is required to believe in them.

Whatever question one may ask about freedom in a philosophical sense—what is it, finally? and how is it possible in a world of cause and effect?—we know that it comes in degrees. Thus the aforementioned urbanite is *more free* than his provincial cousin. And the modern city dweller, equipped with democratic rights, credit cards, and a television set (each of which embodies a multitude of choices), is empirically *more free* than his Hellenistic predecessor. One should not, of course, read modern individualism and liberties back into the Hellenistic world. But neither should one overlook what all pluralistic situations have in common:

namely a degree of freedom, therefore a degree of solitariness, and therefore an existential position from
which choices—including acts of faith—can be made.

Let us return to our liturgical reformers, who
changed the "I" to a "we" in the creedal affirmations.
Neither ancient Israel nor the early Christian church
were free associations of individuals in a modern sense.
Both were rather *covenantal communities*. The individual
belonged to the first by virtue of birth, to the second by
virtue of baptism. And for both the ancient Israelite and
the early Christian the act of faith occurred within a
communal rather than an individualistic situation. This
argument, while valid to a point, overlooks a few
things. Among others, it overlooks the patriarch Abraham and the apostle Paul. Both figures, one paradigmatic for the old covenant and the other for the new,
represent sharp ruptures with communal solidarity.
Abraham left his community in answer to the call of an
utterly foreign God. Can there be a more solitary, a
more profoundly "individualistic" act, than Abraham's
response to God's command: "Go from your country
and your kindred and your father's house?" To be sure,
what followed was this God's covenant with "a great
nation"; but at the origin of this covenant was an act of
faith by a solitary individual. As to Paul, the immediate
consequence of his encounter with the risen Christ on
the road to Damascus was to tear him, radically and
painfully, out of the community in which he had previously invested his entire being. Again, what followed
was a new covenant based on baptism understood as
an act of God rather than of men. But let it not be overlooked that the early Christians, living in the midst of a
religious pluralism strongly resembling our own, *chose*
to be baptized. The faith of ancient Israel constituted
one of the great historic breaks out of archaic commu-

nity, and the faith of the early Church further radical-
ized this break in its separation of the covenant from the
accident of an individual's birth. Even when the Church
instituted the baptism of infants, the liturgy surrounding this ceremony maintained the fiction (empirically
speaking) that the infant chose to be baptized.

If Abraham and Paul were very early prototypes of
modern individualism in the biblical tradition, perhaps
one could speak of a "proto-individualism"—that is,
not what we mean by individualism today, but its first
beginnings—of which Socrates and possibly even Ulys-
ses might be considered parallel examples. Be this as it
may, modernization has brought a quantum leap both
in pluralization and individuation. The pluralization extends from the material level all the way into the sphere
of ideas and values. Technology immensely increases
the choice of tools by which the environment is transformed, the market economy multiplies lifestyle choices
as democracy multiplies political ones, and urbanization creates a milieu in which a multitude of moral and
religious options open up. *Modernity is a gigantic movement from fate to choice in the human condition.* One can
argue that some of these choices are trivial, and also
that this increase in freedom comes at a price. All the
same, the individual in the modern pluralistic situation
not only has the opportunity to choose; he is *compelled*
to choose. Since less and less can be taken for granted,
the individual cannot fall back on firmly established
patterns of behavior and thought; willy-nilly, he must
opt for one possibility rather than another. Thus he becomes a free agent in a way that, at best, was much
more difficult in most earlier periods of history. Life becomes *a project*—more accurately, a series of projects—
and so, in a truly revolutionary way, does the individual's worldview and identity. The phrase "a self-made

man," presumably derived from the vocabulary of free enterprise, has a meaning reaching far beyond the sphere of economic behavior.

Jean-Paul Sartre proposed that man is condemned to freedom. This key proposition of existential philosophy was intended as a general description of the human condition. As such it might be empirically questioned— was a Stone Age hunter condemned to be free? But as a particular description of the condition of *modern* man it is remarkably accurate. The modern situation forces individuals to make a multitude of free choices, many of them admittedly banal. The same situation also makes possible choices of high deliberation and seriousness, the kind that Sartre and the other existentialists had in mind. It is of some importance to see that these weighty choices, including Pascal's wager and Kierkegaard's leap of faith, come out of the same subsoil that compels the many trivial choices of life in a modern society. In this sense (with due apologies to other schools of philosophers), we are all condemned to be existentialists.

Now, modern society is obviously not an agglomeration of isolated individuals making desperate choices as if they were actors in a Sartrean play. There is far more real community in evidence than the critics of modernity think. Modern America has developed a particular genius for creating every variety of community within the context of a pluralistic, individualistic, and mobile society. Increasingly, though, these communities too are *chosen,* and this makes them very different from the communities in which individuals were born and sentenced to live until death. This point was nicely illustrated in the debate that followed the publication of Michael Novak's book *The Unmeltable Ethnics,* which some welcomed as heralding the putative ethnic renascence of the 1970s in America. Critics pointed out that most Americans did not seem to feel any great obligation to keep up the ethnic traditions of their immigrant forefathers. Novak responded by saying that ethnicity could now be freely chosen. He was right, of course; but clearly, when this happens, ethnicity means something very different from what it meant in the past. Compare an American who, for whatever reasons, decides to rediscover his ethnic roots with the meaning ethnicity has in the Middle East. In the first case, ethnicity is a project freely undertaken by an individual, who would be quite free to choose instead a project of religious conversion or sexual reorientation. In the second case, ethnicity is an inexorable fate, often a tragic one, about which the individual has little if any choice. There is, of course, no question as to which type of ethnic community is stronger.

Those who deplore the alienations of modernity are on good empirical ground. Modern man is indeed more solitary than most of his ancestors. But by the same token, and for exactly the same reasons, modern man is more free. If one deplores the alienation, one is implicitly deploring the freedom. Conversely, if one values the freedom, the alienation is a cost one must accept. When it comes to the religious implications of modernization, one ought to decide whether free allegiance to a creed is preferable to an allegiance into which an individual is socialized, as he is with other taken-for-granted patterns of behavior and thought. If in our faith we are children of Abraham and Paul, it seems to me we should welcome rather than deplore the new freedom of modernity.

This does not change the fact that the situation of modernity, experienced by some as a great liberation, is experienced by others (often the very same individuals) as a great burden. This was so when modernization began in Europe. It is visibly so today when modernization has become a worldwide revolution. It is an exhilarating experience for some to be liberated from the ancient bonds of family, clan, tribe, village, or caste. The same liberation can also be experienced as a terrible threat—as being thrown out into a world in which one is alone, unprotected, with all one's beliefs and one's very identity continually put in question. This is why there have been from the beginning and continue to be today powerful movements of counter-modernization. "Back to the ways of our ancestors!" is the typical slogan of these movements. Sometimes they succeed, but usually only for short periods of time, or alternatively in small, tightly controlled reservations—so-called "intentional communities." Modernization is a phenomenon of awesome power, not quite irresistible but nearly so. For example, it is instructive to recall that the purpose of the Meiji Restoration in nineteenth-century Japan was to resist the threat of modern Western imperialism and to preserve the traditional values of Japanese society. The slogan of this movement was "Revere the emperor, expel the barbarians!" It was under this slogan that the Meiji regime launched the modernization of Japan, one of the most dramatic transformations in recent history. It began with a call for the authority of tradition; it led in a more or less straight line to the little miracles of modern technology rolling off the assembly lines of Toyota, Hitachi, or Mitsubishi. As to keeping modernity at bay by locking oneself up in tight little enclaves, this too is very difficult. Ask an Amish farmer in Pennsylvania or a Hasidic rabbi in the Williamsburg section of Brooklyn.

Since modern freedom and modern solitariness are inevitably linked, the flight from one necessarily involves flight from the other. Erich Fromm (leaving aside his doubtful psychoanalytic assumptions) neatly caught this reality when he spoke of an "escape from freedom." He coined that phrase in an attempt to explain the attractiveness of totalitarian ideologies. But totalitarianism is only the most extreme form of a quest for community (in Robert Nisbet's phrase). This quest has taken many different forms in recent history, both in the West where modernity originated and in other parts of the world into which it has spread. There are movements of cultural traditionalism, of religious fundamentalism, or of ideological collectivism, all seeking to reintegrate the individual in a secure, all-encompassing community—and, necessarily, thereby revoking the freedom which cannot survive in such a community, even if this community was freely chosen in the beginning. Nationalism has in all likelihood been the most important ideological and political vehicle for this quest in modern times. The nation presents itself as an all-embracing community. It frequently succeeds in making this plausible to significant numbers of people when it is first invented (all nations are inventions, some more recent than others). When nationalism has attained its political goal—the nation-state—the claim to community rapidly loses plausibility. Other, less political forms of the quest for community then come to the fore in terms of religion, voluntary associations, lifestyles, or even sexual experimentation.

In considering the quest for community in contemporary America, it is useful to distinguish between those communal constructions that respect modern individualism and those that regard it as a perversion to be overcome. The former type, of course, stand in that long tradition of American voluntary associations which de Tocqueville already perceived and admired, and which then as now includes most organized religion. The latter type ranges across a wide spectrum of ideological contents—religious, political, aesthetic, and other. All of them promise to deliver the individual from his solitariness or "excessive individualism" and receive him into the embrace of a salvific community. In the process, the individual "discovers" (or invents) himself in the new communal identity. Almost all religious traditions are quite capable of performing this trick and there are groups within all the major denominations (in addition to numerous sectarian or cult groupings) that perform it successfully. Whether the new identity is then reinforced by prayer breakfasts, recitals of the rosary, or studying Talmud may be significant theologically; it makes little difference in terms of the social-psychological rewards. The same communal embrace is available in secular versions—black brotherhood, feminist sisterhood, revolutionary comradeship, and so on; similar satisfactions are also available in politically conservative packages.

Given the realities of a modern society, there is a good deal of self-delusion in all-these communal identities. This form of self-delusion is a very precise case of what Sartre called "bad faith": A free act is reinterpreted as a necessary fate. Thus the great metamorphosis appears to be reversed: One moves again from a world of choices into a world of fate. But this move is itself an act of choice, and it could be reversed by another act of choice. The individual who makes such a move can pretend that this is not so, but deep down he knows it. This becomes especially clear in cases where the new communal identity actually claims to be a community based on birth, similar to most pre-modern identities. Thus a secular American Jew (perhaps even one of mixed ethnic background) may be converted to one of the more communalistic versions of Orthodox Judaism and in the process "discover" himself as a Jew. This "discovery" purports to be an acknowledgment of a Jewish destiny, indeed is often loudly proclaimed as such. But the individual who undergoes this conversion knows all the time that it was he as an individual who *chose* to identify with this alleged destiny, in specific actions that he can remember well, and he also knows that it is within his power to reverse those actions. This contradiction between an ideology of peoplehood and a social reality of voluntary allegiances has been a major problem for Judaism in America, but other groups, both religious and secular, face similar problems when they present themselves as to-be-taken-for-granted truth. One can be "born again"; one can also, alas, be "*un*born." One can choose to define oneself as an "ontological" Catholic, but that ontology must be renewed in an ongoing sequence of deliberate choices.

The aforementioned change in the language of the creeds is only part of a larger communalistic thrust by our liturgical reformers. In the Catholic as well as the other liturgical churches, the traditional "sacrificial position" of the officiant was reversed: He now no longer stands before the altar, looking outward from the congregation, but rather stands *behind* the altar, looking *at* the congregation. An observation was made to me not long after Vatican II by a Catholic acquaintance who said that the new position was strongly reminiscent of a bartender at work; he cited this among several reasons why he could no longer bear to go to mass. This new position makes wonderfully clear that the sacred being that is worshiped exists not *outside* the gathered community but rather *inside* it. It is a powerful symbolic reversal. I suppose that liturgists can cite any number of ancient antecedents to justify the change. Who knows what motivated some bishop in seventh-century Antioch or ninth-century Lyons to insist that priests should face the congregation while celebrating the eucharist? In twentieth-century America there is the strong suggestion that what is happening here is a community worshiping itself. I strongly suspect that most of the time this is exactly what is happening. From a biblical point of view, what is happening is a form of idolatry.

One could go on: To the embarrassed handshakes mislabeled "the kiss of peace." To the preacher mounting the pulpit in full sacerdotal regalia, only to begin his sermon with a hearty "good morning." To the dedicated removal of every vestige of poetic beauty from the language of the liturgy, as was done by the people who translated the Anglican Book of Common Prayer, one of the great monuments of the English language, into prose resembling that of a mail-order catalogue. I think that what all these changes add up to is the statement that nothing extraordinary is going on, that what is happening is a gathering of ordinary people enjoying the experience of community. Where the liturgy has also been politicized—as in the recent translation of the liturgy and Scripture into feminist idiom—the redefinition of worship as a communal celebration is further reinforced; but the redefinition can also occur without it.

It seems to me that all of this reflects a serious mistake about the nature of worship. All true worship is a difficult attempt to reach out for transcendence. It is this reaching *out* that must be symbolized, by whatever resources a particular tradition has at hand. The chosen form will certainly have a communal aspect. But the community itself is not the object of the exercise; at best it is the subject. I further think that in the Christian case, the religious community is what Wolfhart Pannenberg has called "proleptic": The congregation itself is not what matters, but the community of the Kingdom of God which the gathered congregation feebly foreshadows. Nor is this proleptic community contained within the walls of a particular sanctuary: It includes the community of the living everywhere, and of the living and the dead; ultimately it includes the worshiping community of the angels and all creation.

I suppose human beings have always had a problem about how to relate their feeble gestures of worship with the eternal choir of the angels. In earlier times this problem was solved (if one can speak of a solution) by the community of which the individual was a more or less insignificant member. The problem takes on a much sharper form by the solitary believer in the modern situation. This again raises the question as to whether this solitary view must be overcome before we can reach out to the transcendent.

Which is the true self? Is it the individual alone, divested as far as possible from all social roles and communal attachments? Or is it, on the contrary, the individual within these roles and attachments? And does the question about a true self even make any sense at all?

The human mind has grappled with these questions for many centuries, and not only in the West. An argument could be made, for example, that the entire course of philosophical reflection in India, all the way back to the Vedas, revolved around these questions. Modern Western thought has not resolved them either. On the one hand, as we previously observed, the advent of modernity has greatly sharpened the process of individuation and in consequence has given greater credence to the idea of the authentic self as autonomous, indeed solitary. On the other hand, the tendency of both philosophy and the human sciences (biological, psychological, and social) in this century has been in the other direction: Mach's previously quoted dictum about the "unsalvageable self" quite neatly summarizes this tendency. Certainly the social sciences do not give much support to the notion of a self detached from roles and attachments. Yet there remains the irresistible conviction within the consciousness of individuals that there is indeed such a self, a conviction that surfaces most clearly in the area of moral judgments: Just reflect on the consequences for our conception of human rights if the idea of an autonomous self were abandoned.

I doubt very much whether the issue can be resolved by means of either philosophical reflection or scientific evidence. It is probably one of those questions that must in the end be left to what Pascal called "the reason of the heart"—not a very reliable authority, but no less reliable than the endless antinomies of theoretical reason. I am also inclined to think that the idea of a self over and beyond all socializations can only be maintained in a view of reality that includes transcendence. Dostoyevsky proposed that if God does not exist, everything is permitted. The proposition could be paraphrased: If God does not exist, any self is possible—and the question as to which of the many possible selves is "true" becomes meaningless. Existential philosophy, most of it based on atheistic assumptions, has quite logically drawn from this insight the conclusion that the self is a matter of decision.

I strongly suspect that in a worldview that denies or brackets transcendence, the negative conclusions about the self arrived at by various strands of recent philosophy are quite plausible. The existentialists are not alone here. Mention has already been made of Ernst Mach, whose rejection of the notion of the self was

translated by the novelist Robert Musil (who, before becoming a novelist, wrote a philosophical thesis about
Mach) into the statement that the self is a big hole,
which people then fill with a lot of activity in order to
cover it up. The post-modernist theories about the self
as nothing but a social construction, with nothing
"given" at the core, belong to the same broad development of what can very accurately be described as the
deconstruction of the self. In the absence of any transcendent rootage of the self, perhaps the most that can
be said is that the self, which is never a given, can perhaps be a difficult achievement, an act of the will by
which individuals, always in collaboration with other
human beings, create themselves. In other words, there
can be no self without God.

Be this as it may, the historical fact remains that one
of the fundamental roots of the idea and (more important) the experience of the solitary self in the West is to
be found in ancient Israel; to the extent that the Hebrew
Bible continues to be an authority for contemporary
Christians and Jews, this fact ought to have some
weight. I think it can be shown that a particular crystal-
lization of the self took place in confrontation with the
biblical God. The religion of ancient Israel radically rel-
ativized or abolished outright that whole continuum of
beings that united the individual with the cosmos in the
mythological matrix; in doing so, it brought about a
sharp polarization between an utterly transcendent God
and the human individual to whom God speaks. This
polarization *isolates* the individual—perhaps not in comparison with modern man, but certainly in comparison
with the mythological world out of which God called
Israel. There turned out to be enormous ethical implications to this proto-individuation. It is very clearly expressed in the dramatic confrontation between King

David and the prophet Nathan recounted in the twelfth chapter of the Second Book of Samuel. David had caused the murder of Bathsheba's husband in order to incorporate her in his harem—a perfectly acceptable expression of royal prerogative in terms of oriental conceptions of kingship. After Nathan cleverly leads David to condemn a man who shows no pity in destroying what another man loves, the prophet tells David that he is just such a man—"You are the man." This sentence sovereignly ignores all the communal legitimations of kingship in the ancient Near East. Indeed, it ignores all the social constructions of the self as understood at that time. It passes normative judgment on David the man—a naked man, a man divested of all the trappings of community, *a man alone.* I believe that this view of the relation between God and man, and therefore among men, continues to be normative for a Christian understanding of the human condition.

Biblical religion defines man as *responsible,* in both meanings of the English word, etymological and conventional. Man is he who can respond to God—that, and only that, is his "true self." As Luther once put it: Man exists by virtue of God's address, and he exists as long as God continues to address him. Let me pass by here the wonderfully economical way in which Luther sums up in this statement both the core of a Christian anthropology and the central reason why Christians may hope for eternal life. But further: Because man is a being addressed by God and called upon to respond, man is also ethically accountable. Unless we can conceive of an autonomous individual, it is meaningless to ascribe moral responsibility to human beings; indeed, the very notion of moral responsibility becomes meaningless. But David, the solitary man standing before God, is also the man who can be made accountable for his actions.

There are the other questions I posed some way back, and it is quite possible to reflect about them without immediate reference to the biblical tradition or indeed any religious view of the world: Was Western history a big mistake? Is modernity the biggest mistake?

If a mistake is thought to be anything that falls out of a statistically normal pattern, then the West in general and Western-derived modernity in particular have certainly been mistakes. The Dutch historian Jan Romein coined the phrase "the common human pattern" to denote some features of society and culture that can be found throughout history. The modern West deviates sharply from this common pattern, not least in the character and degree of individuation. This is the sound empirical foundation for the claim that Western individualism is an aberration; the common pattern has the individual tightly bonded within his community. The claim of an aberration has, of course, been made both by observers standing outside the Western tradition and by critics from within it—by Asian philosophers, for instance, and by Marxist ones. They will, of course, differ as to the kind of community that would save us from this perverse predicament, but they will find much to agree with in their description of the predicament itself.

Fortunately or unfortunately, truth and error cannot be determined by statistical means. The overwhelming majority of human beings in the past, and quite possibly even today, have believed in demonic possession. Nevertheless, I am inclined to disagree. Has Western individualism been a terrible mistake? I think not: both because of the valuable ideas that have derived from it, but also because of the living experiences that this individuation has made possible. Both the ideas and the experiences are intricately linked to freedom. For Western individualism, like no other worldview in human history, has proposed (I would say *discovered*) the irreplaceable worth of every individual, regardless of race, nation, gender, age, physical or mental handicap, belief system, *or any other collective ascription*. Every human culture recognizes certain rights belonging to an individual by virtue of his membership in a community. Only Western individualism has brought about the recognition of an individual's rights *apart from* his community and, if necessary, *against* it. These rights are closely linked to a perception of the individual as a free and responsible being, indeed a solitary being—and not just an agent of some communal entity.

Are we prepared to revise our view of what is ethically permissible between human beings in accordance with a communalistic anthropology? Are we prepared to do so even knowing what human horrors such anthropologies have served to legitimate in our own century? I know that I am not.

But the free individual, free even to stand against the community, is not simply an idea: Numerous human beings experience themselves in such freedom. As I suggested before, this experience is not always agreeable. Various burdens accompany emancipation from any community, especially one to which we have long-lasting and deep attachments. For those of us who have experienced ourselves in freedom, these anthropological questions are not just matters of theoretical interest. They touch upon an understanding of what we are and where we have come from. If I have once experienced myself as a free individual, I can of course later on entertain the hypothesis that this experience was based on illusion. But I am not willing to accept this hypothesis. I prefer to remain faithful to my experience—if you will, to *keep faith* with it. (This is not the same faith spoken of in the Christian creeds; but it is faith all the same.)

This, then, is the meaning I would assign to the subject of the first sentence of the Nicene Creed: The solitary "I" is here affirming this belief, the "I" over and beyond all collective or communal assignments—the "I" alone with reality and alone with God. This is not to deny the importance of social ties and social locations (were I to do so, I would have to resign my commission as a sociologist). It is simply to say that, as I confront the meaning of my life, all this social world fades away to insignificance. In modern literature I can think of no more trenchant expression of this insight than Tolstoy's novella "The Death of Ivan Ilyich." I can think of no more succinct summation that Simone Weil's (in her collection of essays *Gravity and Grace*) *"Society is the cave. The way out is solitude."* Indeed, Weil can be said to be paradigmatic for the solitary believer in the modern situation. Her life is one long story of marginality. She was intensely patriotic as a Frenchwoman during World War II, but she was deeply suspicious of any communal solidarities. She was Jewish, but she rejected not only Judaism but any secular form of Jewish identity. Personally awkward and idiosyncratic, she went to Spain to serve on the republican side in the civil war, only to be sent home after an embarrassing accident. After the German occupation of France she went to England as a refugee and, although in perpetual ill health, refused to eat more than the minimal food ration allowed in France—a decision that caused her final illness. And while in hiding from the Germans she was converted to Catholicism, but refused to be baptized because she did not want to distance herself from the sufferings of the Jews, but also because she rejected what she considered the false comforts of Catholic communalism. To be sure, Simone Weil represents an extreme, an eccentric case of the solitary believer. Her case, however, may also be seen as paradigmatic.

The posture I'm describing here does not idealize the modern pluralistic situation. It is emphatically not based on any myth of progress, on the notion that modernity is thus far the highest stage of human evolution. Modernity, like any historical moment, is very mixed, and includes specific elements that I, for one, would view as retrogressive. But it happens to be the situation in which we find ourselves. We should not deny it, or delude ourselves that we are somewhere else. To accept this situation means accepting what I have elsewhere called the "heretical imperative," namely the fact that it forces us to make choices. But to say that we ought simply to accept the modern situation is too pejorative. Not everything about this situation deserves to be deplored. And above all, as I have tried to argue, the modern situation has brought us an unprecedented freedom.

Excursus:
Robert Musil and the
Salvage of the Self

To have a self is an essential human quality across all the differences of history and cultures. Yet each age and each society modifies this anthropologically constant figure, to give birth to "Hellenic man," or to the "Chinese mind," or to *homo hierarchicus*, and so on. In each of these cases, a prime analytic problem is the delineation between that underlying self, which all human beings have always possessed, and the historically specific self that is the construction of an age and a society.

A good case can be made that literature, and especially the specifically modern form of literature that is the novel, may well offer the best guide to the delineation of modern Western individuality. This, obviously, is not the place to make that case. But one example from the argument can be explored—an example important and persuasive enough to make one optimistic about the outcome of a more comprehensive demonstration. The example is that of Robert Musil (1880–1942), the Austrian novelist whose work is slowly winning recognition. Indeed, Musil's major novel, *Der Mann ohne Eigenschaften* (*The Man without Qualities*), on which he worked for some twenty years but left unfinished at his death, has as one of its explicit central themes the question of the modern self, a question to which Musil brought not only his great gifts as a writer but also his background (probably unusual in modern Western literature) as a professional philosopher.

Like Ulrich, the protagonist of *The Man without Qualities*, Musil in his youth was a man of shifting careers. Brought up in a military school (immortalized in his first novel, *Young Toerless*), Musil became an officer in the Austro-Hungarian army, strongly disliked this way of life (at least for himself—he always retained a lingering respect for it), and resigned his commission. He went to study engineering at the technical university in Bruenn (today's Brno, in Czechoslovakia), where his father was a professor. But engineering did not suit him either. And so, again after successful graduation, Musil went to Berlin to study philosophy, mathematics, and experimental psychology. He obtained his doctorate, with a dissertation on the Austrian philosopher Ernst Mach (often viewed as one of the fathers of the Vienna School and of neopositivism in general—curiously, Mach inspired Lenin to write his only philosophical treatise). Only then did Musil decide to devote himself entirely to writing. Until the end of his life, he wrote under mostly penurious circumstances as a refugee from nazism in Geneva, the town (as he was very conscious of) that brought forth Jean-Jacques Rousseau, father of modern subjectivism, and that in the 1930s and 1940s was already marked by the abstract internationalism that characterizes it today—a place of hotels full of strangers with indeterminate nationalities.

During his years in Berlin, and in order to be helpful to a friend who experimented in optical perception,

Musil invented a laboratory gadget that he patented under the name *"Variationskreisel,"* or "variation wheel" (it was apparently designed to experiment with the perception of colors, and Musil hoped, wrongly, that he would make money on it). The name would fit perfectly the structure of Musil's major novel, which contains an ever-shifting kaleidoscope of social worlds, roles and personalities, ideas and worldviews; indeed, a good argument has been made by Goetz Mueller to the effect that Musil intended the novel to be a comprehensive critique of existing ideologies. The subject of Musil's doctoral dissertation is equally relevant to the novel. One of Mach's most influential propositions, as noted earlier, was that the classical (especially the Cartesian) notion of the self can no longer be maintained—the proposition of the "non-salvageable self" (*das unrettbare Ich*). *The Man without Qualities* is one extended effort at salvage.

The action of the novel occurs within the space of one year, from August 1913 to August 1914, ending with the outbreak of World War I. Ulrich, the protagonist, is a man in his early thirties, a mathematician who interrupts a successful career abroad to return to Austria for a year. He intends to take a year's "vacation from life," as he calls it, in order to get to the bottom of a vague feeling of dissatisfaction with his life and to discover how he can best apply his considerable talents. More or less by accident he becomes involved with a patriotic project (called the *Parallelaktion*, because it is initiated in response to a similar undertaking in Germany) designed to prepare the celebration, in 1918, of the seventieth anniversary of the coronation of the Emperor Franz Joseph. On this occasion the true meaning of the Austro-Hungarian state is to be proclaimed to the world, and the work of the project is to figure out just what that meaning is. The reader, of course, is aware of

the ironic fact that the year 1918 was to see not the proclamation of the true meaning of Austria-Hungary but its
cataclysmic destruction. Later in the year Ulrich's father
(a professor of law at a provincial university) dies, and
on that occasion Ulrich is reunited with his estranged
sister Agathe. The two siblings decide to live together
in Vienna in order to pursue the mystical quest for "the
other condition" to which both have become committed. The posthumous materials of the novel allow no
certain conclusion as to whether Musil intended this
quest to succeed or fail.

Ulrich (like Musil) is convinced that one cannot acquire the perspective of modern science and go on looking at the world as one previously had. What is more,
no solution to the problems of human life (political,
moral, even religious) that ignores the scientific perspective is tenable. The opening paragraph of the novel
gives the precise weather report for Europe, with all the
antiseptic language of meteorology, ironically ending
with the summation that it was a beautiful August day
of the year 1913. The tension between scientific exactitude and the wealth of the subjective emotional meanings implied in the last sentence could not be more
graphically expressed. In the text, the last sentence is
half-apologetically introduced with the statement that it
is "somewhat old-fashioned." Yet virtually everything
in human life that has subjective value can be so described; indeed the self, or rather the idea we have of
it, is "somewhat old-fashioned." One might put the
question, without violating Musil's intention, whether
a good meteorologist can actually have a self or not.

The definition of the scientific method (Ulrich, incidentally, endlessly explains all this to Agathe and to
various other interlocutors) is that reality is broken up
into component parts which are then perceived as in-

teracting in causal chains. In other words, what was
once perceived as a whole now comes to be perceived
as a system of variables. This same process of disinte-
gration applies to the self. Put differently, it becomes
more and more difficult to see the self as the center of
the individual's actions. Instead, these actions come to
be perceived as events that happen to the individual,
separate from himself, explainable in terms of both external (social) and internal (organic and psychic) causes.
The Cartesian self, which was capable of pronouncing
"cogito ergo sum," is dissolved in a Machian flux of ob-
jectivities. Modern subjectivity, as it were, eviscerates
itself.

   This perception is sharply developed with two
characters in the novel, one insane to begin with, the
other in the process of going insane. The first character
is Moosbrugger, a demented simpleton who is on trial
for the apparently senseless murder of a prostitute and
in whose fate Ulrich develops a passing interest. It may
be remarked that Musil's lengthy descriptions of Moosbrugger's perceptions of himself and of the world are
masterpieces of clinical imagination. Moosbrugger is a
simple, friendly man, liked by everyone (including his
jailers), who suddenly erupts into homicidal frenzy.
Who is the true Moosbrugger and what motivates him?
The lawyers at his trial, the consulting psychiatrists,
and Ulrich must all ask this question. At his trial the
court tries hard to understand him as an acting person.
The court has no other option, since it must determine
whether, under the law, Moosbrugger can be held accountable for his actions (it so happens that Ulrich's father wrote his *magnum opus* on the concept of accountability in the legal thought of Pufendorf). But these
efforts at understanding Moosbrugger as an acting person are in total contrast with Moosbrugger's self-expe-

rience, in which everything, including his own actions, just happens to him and in which he remains "eternally innocent." The main reason why Ulrich is interested in this case is his strong suspicion that allegedly normal people are really not very different from Moosbrugger in this self-experience. Perhaps there is no "true" Moosbrugger—and no "true" Ulrich either.

The other character is Clarisse, wife of an old friend of Ulrich's, a brilliantly gifted musician, who is also strongly drawn to Moosbrugger (she wants to liberate him from prison because she senses that he is musical) and who eventually descends into madness herself. On one occasion Clarisse visits a mental hospital in which Moosbrugger is being examined. The narrator observes that many people are afraid of madness because it would mean losing themselves—madness, that is, reminds even normal people of the precariousness of what they cherish as their self. One of the patients salutes Clarisse as the seventh son of the Emperor and stubbornly refuses to accept her denial. In rising panic she discovers that she is quite prepared to believe him, and she and her companions leave the hospital without having seen Moosbrugger. The question here is a variation of the earlier one: Who is the true Clarisse and why is she going mad?

In this perspective, madness is a liberating simplification, because the madman is paradoxically much more certain of who he is than the allegedly sane individual. The quest for the true nature of things is replicated throughout the earlier part of the novel by the patriotic project. The question here, of course, is: What is the true Austria? The chairman of the project, Count Leinsdorf, a deeply pious and at the same time deeply skeptical aristocrat, is convinced that everything and everyone has a true nature; he is also convinced that, intuitively, he knows what these true entities are. Resting in this (certainly very "old-fashioned") certitude, he can afford to preside over a committee of quarreling intellectuals, each of whom has a different view of reality. He does not expect any interesting insights from this ideological pandemonium; his approach to the enterprise is purely tactical and political. Even if his certitude is finally based on illusion, Musil conveys the impression that Leinsdorf is a lucky man. (So, incidentally, is the representative of the war ministry, General Stumm von Bordwehr, a character drawn by Musil with very great sympathy.) But the order of the state is about to disintegrate as the order of the self has disintegrated in Moosbrugger and Clarisse, and the coming war will be a collective madness—infinitely more murderous than Moosbrugger's and yet, at least initially, experienced as a great liberation (one of the plans for the novel was to end it with a description of the enormous enthusiasm with which the outbreak of war was greeted in Austria as in the other belligerent countries on both sides).

The idea that the self is some sort of central entity, and that every individual therefore has a "true" self, is an illusion. Perhaps an individual may, through great effort, acquire such a center; but it does not exist as a given of human nature. Rather, the self is a "hole" which must somehow be "filled," both by oneself and by others. This reciprocal enterprise of endowing individuals with definable identities is described especially in the relationship between Ulrich and Agathe (again with great psychological precision, which is strongly reminiscent of George Herbert Mead's description of the social genesis of the self). In practice, for most people, the best way to "fill" this "hole" is by means of action (in Meadian terms, the individual performs his socially assigned roles, and the aggregate of these roles constitutes what he "is"). For those people who fancy themselves to have a "soul" (intellectuals, poets, those with a sense for the "finer things"), there is another method. In the words of a chapter heading, "ideals and morality are the best means to fill the big hole that one calls soul." The implication, of course, is that it matters little *which* ideas or *which* morality are employed to this end.

Early on in his participation in the patriotic project, Ulrich suggests that there ought to be "a general secretariat for exactitude and soul," to provide guidance for people in the quandary of combining these two ideas. One surmises that this suggestion for a sort of ministry of general psychotherapy is only half-facetious. The intellectuals associated with the project discuss the Marxist and psychoanalytical theories about the true foundation of human action, that substructure (*Unterbau*) which, if one only knew what it was, would explain everything. But, of course, they all disagree, leading Leinsdorf to complain about the unreliability of the people in the superstructure—a statement wonderfully summarizing his disdain for the intellectuals, his misunderstanding of the theories at issue, and his unshakable confidence in the reliability of the old order. Clearly, it would not be easy to carry out Ulrich's suggestion.

The novel is full of ruminations about the problem of order—or, more accurately, the problem of ordering. The patriotic project is to legitimate the order of the state. Moosebrugger understands his acts of violence as desperate attempts to restore order to his world (at one point he himself is described as "an escaped parable of order"). The only order that Clarisse knows is that of music, and Ulrich finds solace in the cool order of mathematics. In one conversation Ulrich, only half-ironically, explains to General Stumm that the military is the most spiritual of all institutions, because spirit is order, and who can deny that the military is the most orderly institution, down to the exact spaces between the buttons on an officer's tunic? In the same way, there are various ways of trying to order the self, to somehow fixate it in a way that makes sense. The law (to which Ulrich's father has devoted his life) is the most important "official" agency for this ordering of the self. In one episode Ulrich is caught in a political altercation on the street and is briefly arrested. During his interrogation at a police station, where he is asked about his age, profession, and the like, with no regard for all the allegedly "finer" aspects of his existence, Ulrich experiences a "statistical disenchantment" of his person—and, strangely (or, in Musil's perspective, not so strangely), finds a certain satisfaction in this experience. Psychiatry, using categories different from, even contradictory to, those of the law, also seeks to impose some sort of order on the self. All these efforts, though, are ultimately illusionary. They are, in Musil's term, "utopian"—literally nowhere. The self is and remains an unfillable "hole." Yet there also remains the profound urge, and perhaps the possibility, of finding a self that will be (precisely) "reliable." The quest for "the other condition," whatever its religious or metaphysical components, is also the quest for a coherent, ontologically real self. Musil may have been unsure to the end whether that quest was not "utopian" too, but evidently he was unwilling to conclude that it was. In any case, if such a "true" self was possible, it would not be a given, a *datum*, but rather something to be attained, achieved as the result of an enormously difficult effort.

Possibly the self always has been a "hole," but in earlier times people were less aware of this; or perhaps this species of what could be called *Lochmensch* (*homo lacuna*?) is an anthropological innovation of the modern age. Be this as it may, the title of the novel deliberately and self-consciously points to what Musil understood to be a central feature of modern man. Ulrich is first characterized as "a man without qualities" by Walter, Clarisse's husband, who is very critical of this aspect of his old friend. Walter feels that this is a new type of human being created by our age; this type can now be seen in millions of cases. Walter goes on to say that people today (with the exception of Catholic clergy) no longer look like what they are. Ulrich is supposed to be a mathematician. But what does a mathematician look like? At best, he looks generally intelligent, but this does not express any particular content. Ulrich seems to have many qualities, but really he has none. "Nothing is firm for him," everything may be changed again, and he has no idea what he is as a whole. (To which description Clarisse replies, to Walter's intense irritation, that this is precisely what she likes about Ulrich.) It follows from this that, in Musil's words, the man without qualities is *ipso facto* the man of *possibilities*. In other words, the modern self is characterized by its open-endedness, its being-in-process—or, one might venture, by its high degree of freedom. That freedom (if that is what it should be called) is not necessarily pleasing in actual experience; on the contrary, it can be felt as a burden—as it is felt by Ulrich.

In a later passage, the man without qualities is described as a man whose qualities have somehow become independent of him. Indeed, it seems as if these qualities have more relations with each other than with him. Events just follow each other, as *B* follows *A*, surprising the alleged actor as much or even more than those watching him. This was not always so. In the past, a person was much more certain of himself. To be sure, external dangers may have been greater—natural disasters, disease, and war—but the individual belonged to himself in a much clearer way. These observations could all be subsumed under the proposition of Arnold Gehlen that ancient man had "character," while modern man has "personality." The difference is that, paradoxically, the sociological theorist Gehlen deplored this change, while Musil, the philosopher-turned-*Dichter*, welcomed it, despite all the difficulties it created, as an advance in human self-consciousness.

If Ulrich is a man without qualities, Austria-Hungary (or Kakania, as Musil calls it) may be called a nation without qualities. The linguistic confusion underlying Austro-Hungarian institutions reflects the uncertainty regarding the true nature of the monarchy. In a long satirical excursus, a chapter aptly entitled "A State Which Perished Because of a Speech Defect," Musil elaborates this point. The Hungarian half of the monarchy had a clear national identity, even if this had to be imposed coercively by the Magyars on their various Slavic subject populations (that imposition too, of course, failed in the end). But the Austrian half did not even have a name for itself. Its official name was the "Kingdoms and Lands Represented in the Imperial Parliament." How could anyone identify himself with such a designation? Yet, as Leinsdorf and General Stumm knew very well, there was such a thing as Austrian patriotism—a curious mixture of the archaic (this empire, after all, had been in existence for nearly a millennium) and the ultramodern (a nation-state without a nation, faithfully reflecting the "hole" character of modern man). The patriotic project is designed to remedy the "speech defect" by producing the "true Austrian idea." Leinsdorf is quite suspicious of such a project, though he wants to make use of it politically. He suspects that too much reflection on the nature of the state cannot help but subvert its taken-for-granted order. He is right, of course; political loyalty based upon reflection on an idea is, by definition, fragile and fugitive (Edmund Burke would certainly have sympathized with Leinsdorf). Like all real conservatives, Leinsdorf relies on intuitive certainties rather than intellectual conclusions. His tragedy (and that of Austria-Hungary) is that modern man does not come easily to intuitive certainties; more precisely, he dismantles, by way of reflection, those certainties with which he had to begin. Helmut Schelsky has called this modern propensity "permanent reflectiveness" (*Dauerreflektion*); it is as subversive of the political order ("critical consciousness-raising") as, in the mode of modern psychology, it is subversive of the order of the self. Thus the patriotic project is a *Parallelaktion* in an additional sense; its ideological self-evisceration is parallel to Ulrich's mathematical-scientific disaggregation of the Cartesian self. In Meadian social psychology it is evident that an individual is more real to others than he is to himself—at least, real in the sense of being perceived as a coherent, comprehensible entity. Ironically, it is a foreigner, the Prussian business tycoon and would-be great thinker Arnheim, who seems to have a better grasp of "the Austrian idea" than the native intellectuals.

The political problem of the modern world is that all systems of order are put in question. The geometrically parallel problem of modern personality is that all its systems of order become equally questionable. There is one grand solution to these twin problems, which is the solution of collectivism. In the novel it is represented mainly by the figure of Hans Sepp, a sort of proto-Nazi (who, ironically, is the boyfriend of the Jewish girl Gerda, with whom Ulrich also has a brief and unsatisfactory affair). Sepp and his group of young German nationalists despise Austria-Hungary (later, they try to disrupt the patriotic project which they view as a Slavic plot); they are anti-Semitic because of the alleged intellectualism of the Jews; and Sepp particularly dislikes Ulrich because of his skeptical questioning of every "wholesome" idea. Sepp and his friends find a seemingly reliable collective identity in what they call "national feeling," which Musil contemptuously describes as "that merging of their perpetually quarreling selves in a dreamed unity." But they are not the only ones to find illusionary solace in a "dreamed unity" (*erträumte Einigkeit*) of collective solidarity. In Musil's posthumous materials a minor role is played by a militant socialist, Schmeisser (the German word denotes a machine-pistol), whom Musil describes with equal contempt. Ulrich and Agathe converse in pejorative terms about the false collective identity bestowed by institutional religion as well. And, most important of all, the entire novel moves toward that sublime eruption of "dreamed unity," the ultimate collective madness, which greets the outbreak of war.

The disaggregated modern self is a plural self. The qualities of the person detach themselves from him and become mere appendages of his variable social roles. Early in the novel it is stated that today every individual, not just Ulrich, has at least nine characters— linked consecutively to his vocation, nation, state, class, geographical context, sexuality, consciousness, unconscious mind, and, perhaps, his private life (whatever that means as an additional category)—and, somehow, he must juggle all these characters from day to day. Thus, an individual may be a professor, a Czech, a subject of Austria-Hungary, a person of petit bourgeois antecedents, a lecher, a moralist with an immoralist libido, and on top of that, perhaps, someone with a profound appreciation of art. It is not always easy to keep in motion this menagerie of discrete selves. But then there is also a tenth character, which Musil describes as "the passive fantasy of unfilled spaces" ("*die passive Phantasie unausgefüllter Räume*"). This is the human capacity for "utopian" dreams; all of these dreams, whatever their ideational or normative content, are finally dreams of a self restored to unity, to "wholeness."

One wonders how Musil would have thought of these matters if, instead of being reared on Mach, he had been familiar with Meadian social psychology and its ramifications in the sociology of knowledge. Be this as it may, Musil is aware, though the point is not elaborated much, that the plural self corresponds to a plural social world. Such a world means that an individual must choose. Put differently, the world presents itself to the individual, not as taken-for-granted destiny (the prototypical case through most of history), but rather as specific sets of options. This begins with the most mundane areas of everyday life. When Ulrich acquires a house in Vienna (which later becomes the locale of his mystical experimentation with Agathe), he faces the problem of how to decorate it. He cannot decide on a style. So he decides to leave the choice to his furniture suppliers, as a result of which the house becomes a random and incongruous collection of styles. Here too, in trivial consumer options, the individual hovers between a near-infinity of possibilities.

Yet, upon closer inspection, these mundane options are really not trivial at all. We owe to Ernst Bloch the philosophical concept of "accommodating oneself in the world" (*sich in der Welt einrichten*)—in ordinary German, the word "accommodating" refers to the acquisition of furniture. The individual furnishes his life as he furnishes his house, and very often the latter furniture symbolizes the former. In Ulrich's case, clearly, the disorder of his lodgings is a visible sign of the invisible disorder of his mind. There are, of course, individuals who acquire a "style." They now pretend to superior good taste, to always knowing the right object for the right place, the right gesture for the right occasion. However, these patterns of "wholeness" are social or ideological artifacts. They are, in principle, arbitrary and therefore subject to revision; in the terminology of Alfred Schutz, what we have here are styles "until further notice." By the same token, such styles are "utopian."

The intellectuals in the patriotic project in Musil's novel acquire ideas as Ulrich acquired furniture. Here too there is a bewildering array of choices. Nothing is certain any longer, to be taken for granted. In one of the most hilarious passages in the novel, General Stumm recounts how he tried to put some order into this ideological chaos. Good staff officer that he is, he employs a small platoon of subordinates to draw up a battle plan of ideas. Dominant ideas are shown as advancing armies, there are strategic hillocks of concepts, skirmishes are fought between categorial regiments. Despite these efforts, entered on the map with multicolored pencils (as Stumm learned to do in staff college), an order fails to materialize. The lines between the ideational armies keep shifting, the intellectual generals keep stealing weapons from their opponents and use them to attack their own rear, important categories suddenly disappear, and so on. The general has a deep respect for the life of the mind, but he cannot suppress the mounting suspicion that perhaps the entire battlefield is a sham. He is not so much bothered by the fact that everyone in Diotima's *salon* tells him something different. But, as he explains to Ulrich (who used to be an officer and must therefore have some sense of order), he is troubled by the feeling that the longer he listens to these intellectuals the more they all sound alike. It follows that, in the end, the choice of ideas and moralities is as random as the choice of decorating styles.

The social world allows the individual to choose different careers. Thus Ulrich is, in succession, an officer, a mathematician, and a religio-psychological experimenter. With each possible career go specific roles— and, of course, specific ideas and moralities. Needless to say, this Musilian insight could be vastly elaborated with the use of categories derived from social psychology and the sociology of knowledge. A perfect case of such an analysis of plural roles, with all the appropriate ideational and moral attachments, would be the case of Bonadea, with whom Ulrich has an affair early in the novel. Bonadea is both *une brave bourgeoise*, proper wife and mother, and a wildly roaming nymphomaniac. Somehow she manages to keep both of these discrete social worlds going and segregated from each other. She does feel some unease about this (manifested in very boring self-accusations after each time she has gone to bed with Ulrich), and she has the "utopian" fantasy that somehow, someday, she will integrate the discrepant sides of her being into some sort of "whole." She believes (mistakenly, it turns out) that Diotima commands this "mystery of wholeness," and, in quest of salvation from herself, she insinuates herself into the patriotic project. But then, to her great shock, she discovers that Diotima is having an affair with Arnheim. The high cult of "wholeness" and soul is disclosed to be not very different from the little furtive games of adultery that Bonadea knows all too well. Another "utopia" collapses.

Musil's *The Man without Qualities* is an extraordinarily rich source of insight into the modern self. The insights are not comforting. The self, as traditionally defined in Western civilization (minimally since Descartes) and as still taken for granted in everyday life as well as in the solemn fictions of the law, is disclosed to be an illusion. At its core is a sort of emptiness (strikingly reminiscent of the classical Buddhist conception of *shunyata*). This is what scientific analysis suggests, but the disturbing news is penetrating beyond the small world of scientists. More and more people are uncertain as to who they are, what their motives are or should be, and they are also uncertain as to the true identities and motives of even their most intimate associates. Consequently, there is the pervasive "utopia of the motivated life," as Musil calls it—that is, the dream of a restored unity of self, action, and reality. But all projects to bring this about, individually or collectively, are equally uncertain; to repeat Count Leinsdorf's biting comment, all these people in the superstructure are unreliable—be they philosophers, psychologists, political ideologists (of whatever stripe), or poets. There are still some people walking around in modern society who represent an older mode of being, a traditional "wholeness." Perhaps they are lucky and to be envied. But for those who have drunk of the fountain of modern relativism there does not appear to be a way back. Reactionary restorations are illusionary. So are innovative, "progressive" constructions of "wholeness"; the ultranationalist Sepp and the socialist Schmeisser are mirror images of each other. And the constructions of "wholeness" based on individual eccentricity, in the mode of Clarisse, are likely to end in madness or crime.

Yet Musil is clearly not prepared to give up this utopia of self-realization. Within the logic of the novel, two avenues are left open. One is the skeptical, scientifically reflective, but nevertheless passionate endorsement of modern freedom. The other is the religious quest for the true self revealed in transcendence. There is a secular and a mystical Ulrich, and Musil leaves us in suspense as to which one will prevail at the end of the novel.

The posthumous chapters can be arranged differently. Adolf Frisé, the editor of the standard edition, arranged them in such a way that Ulrich's experiment with "the other condition" fails (after a dramatic journey to Italy, during which he commits incest with Agathe); after this failure Ulrich returns, much sobered but unbroken, to the partial and insecure self-realization of ordinary life. The English translators of the novel have criticized this arrangement of the *Nachlass*, believing that Musil intended the novel to end with the so-called "holy conversations" between brother and sister, thus implying that the religio-mystical experiment had succeeded. A non-specialist examining the Musil opus will incline to the view that Musil himself did not know which outcome to choose. He was clear about one point: There is no secular solution to the "mystery of wholeness." If there is a true self, it can only be revealed as true in a transcendent frame of reference. As suggested before, paraphrasing Dostovevksy, if God does not exist, any self is possible. The dilemma of modern man, but also his challenging opportunity, is that this alternative has become very sharply defined.

5

The Act of Belief

What does it mean to say "I believe" in an affirmation of faith?

Common Christian parlance counter-poses belief
and unbelief, implying that the latter is in some sense a
moral failing, even a betrayal—a sign of ingratitude toward God. There is nothing logically wrong with pair-
ing these terms, though I would resist the generally pejorative implication that goes with the latter: God has
not made it easy for human beings to believe, and the
world provides good grounds for unbelief. I would prefer to pair belief with another, very conventional term—

namely, *knowledge*. Some things I know, and some things I believe; generally speaking, I don't have to believe what I know. Thus I know that $2 + 2 = 4$. It makes little sense to say that I believe this. But if I have before me a closed box containing apples, I may say that I believe it contains *four*; I'm not sure, but I have some reason to think this is the number. In conventional usage, there is a stronger use of the word—as when I say that I believe in democracy, or the integrity of my friend. Here too is a statement about something I don't know, but my belief is something stronger than a probability statement. It is an act that commits me and in which I invest something important, possibly that which is most important. In ordinary usage, of course, it is only this second type of belief that would be graced with the term "faith."

There is a widespread notion that modernity has enormously expanded human knowledge and therefore diminished the area in which belief (or faith) is required. Like most widespread notions, this one has a kernel of truth but is nevertheless false. To be sure, modernity has immensely increased the available body of societal knowledge, as well as what Alfred Schutz called the "stock of knowledge at hand"—that part of the knowledge corpus available to the individual in ordinary, everyday life. But this astronomical expansion of knowledge is virtually all in the area of information about which no act of belief is called for. Thus society has acquired a vast body of knowledge supplied by modern physics, and I in my everyday life know many things of a technological nature (for instance, how to direct-dial a number in Australia) that engineers have distilled from physics for practical use. Nothing in this body of knowledge, however, requires an act of belief, other than in the weaker sense of a probabilistic statement. There are scientists for whom the pursuit of such knowledge is indeed a matter of faith commitment; but this faith precedes rather than follows its actual acquisition; perhaps it is finally a faith in the orderliness of being, which is something that was around for a long time before the advent of modern society. The diffusion of modern scientific and technological styles of thinking has arguably encouraged a pragmatic, rationalistic approach to reality which is averse to faith commitments. This is a common explanation of modern secularity, and it certainly has some validity. But modernity has done something else that contradicts the notion that an expansion of knowledge has reduced the need for belief: Modernity has undermined all taken-for-granted certitudes. And it has done this not because of advances in science and technology, but because of the pluralization of the modern social environment.

The mechanisms by which pluralism accomplishes this demolition have already been discussed. There is nothing mysterious about this. Human beings, due to their intrinsically and inexorably social nature, require social support for whatever they believe about the world. Elsewhere I have employed the concept of "plausibility structure" to denote this dependence on social support: it refers to the particular social context in which a given belief or value is plausible. Thus in rural Guatemala it is plausible to believe in communication with the dead, and in communication with one's unconscious among the American upper middle class. Take an individual out of these social contexts and his beliefs will seem improbable. It follows that beliefs will be more plausible if confirmed with greater unanimity by the believer's community. When virtually everyone supports a particular belief, this belief, no matter what it is, will attain the status of taken-for-granted truth in the individual's mind. In other words, the individual will *know* this alleged truth and will not feel called on to make the effort of faith. Modernization has been giving such plausibility structures a very hard time. Put simply, modernity has created a situation in which certitude is hard to achieve. By this I mean certitude about anything that really matters, as distinct from the physicist's reasonable certitude about some scientific proposition, or my own certitude that, if I dial correctly, I will reach my friend in Melbourne.

If one understands this development, one will no longer be puzzled by the evident fact that this modern age, with all its new knowledge, is as credulous as any in history. For contrary to every commencement speech ever made, education appears to have little if any effect on this modern readiness to believe. There is no imbecility that has not been ardently espoused by some segment of the modern intelligentsia, including some uniquely absurd and invidious superstitions. Indeed, there is some warrant for asserting that the propensity to believe evident nonsense increases rather than decreases with higher education. In this admittedly degraded sense, it can then be said that the modern age has been a great age of belief. Credulity would be a more accurate term.

The modern subversion of taken-for-granted beliefs has affected many areas besides religion. It has severely affected values and moral norms as well as the way individuals define themselves. It is not possible here to discuss these wider effects, but it is important to understand that the difficulties of religious belief in the pluralistic situation are not unique—not due to some mysterious fall from grace—but can be accounted for by clearly identifiable social processes. The acceptance of this view should have the fortunate effect of depriving modern consciousness of the superior cognitive status that has so often been ascribed to it. For well over a hundred years theologians have been trying to accommodate religion to the cognitive requirements of a creature called "modern man," as if it were self-evident that this entity had an enormous epistemological advantage over such characters as the biblical authors or the Church Fathers. In fact, modern man is not a terribly inspiring figure; his much-vaunted rationality is often devoted to projects of little value, and he is chronically insecure about everything, including his own identity. The most positive thing about him, as we have seen, is an unprecedented gift of freedom, and even that he has frequently experienced as a burden to be shed as soon as possible.

Yet I would argue that the modern pluralistic situation, with its negative impact on everything that had previously been taken for granted, has one very great advantage for religious faith: It allows an individual in quest of religious truth to make something of a fresh start. Kierkegaard took the view that, in order to have Christian faith, we must become "contemporaneous" with Jesus. This is a very difficult suggestion. Our pluralistic situation, uncannily similar to that of late Hellenistic and Roman times, gives us a rather interesting opportunity to become "contemporaneous" with the early Church.

The breakdown of taken-for-granted structures of life and thought opens up previously unthinkable possibilities, including the possibility of religious faith. One might put this more strongly by saying that transcendence becomes visible in the breakdown of ordinary reality.

Alfred Schutz has given us painstaking descriptions of what he called "the world taken for granted"—

the collection of ideas and habits that order our everyday lives, but do so *only* if they are, precisely, taken for
granted. In the very moment we begin to question
them, that order is incipiently threatened. Social order
depends upon a collective determination not to question, nor even to reflect upon a large array of assumptions that underlie everyday living. And as Arnold Gehlen has brilliantly argued, social institutions function so
as to allow individuals most of the time to live in a mode
of unreflective spontaneity (if you will, of semi-somno-
lence), without which society would collapse into self-
destructive chaos. From the standpoint of the individual, to live an ordinary life (which also means to take
seriously one's social rules) requires blocking out anything that might rupture the fabric of the ordinary. This
requires considerable effort, but it is not at all impossible for people living reasonably happy lives in a reasonably well-functioning society. If ordinary life is
overcome by either individual or collective catastrophe—bereavement, serious illness, or abrupt loss of social position, or war, revolution, or natural disasters—
then the pretense that all is in order may be shattered.
But even in lives that seem very normal indeed there
will be moments when the taken-for-granted reality will
suddenly be pierced, opening a window on a reality
that is strangely different.

Probably the best-known depiction of such a moment in modern literature is the incident with the *ma-
deleines* in Proust's *Remembrance of Things Past*, when the
world of the protagonist seems suddenly and utterly
transformed in the course of consuming some perfectly
innocent cookies. But I think it is Robert Musil, as discussed in the preceding excursus, who has given us an
almost pedantically full catalogue of cases in which ordinary reality is "abolished" and something terrifyingly

other shines through. There are cases of physical violence, sexual frenzy, the theoretical ecstasies of pure mathematics and the aesthetic ones of music, and even mystical experience. But there are also cases in which the break occurs in the midst of seemingly trivial incidents—as when Musil's protagonist loses his way walking home through nocturnal streets, or when he is suddenly overcome by the absurdity of a set of bureaucratic memoranda he is asked to read. All such experiences explode, if only for an instant, the security we experience in living normally. This security is revealed to be artificial and very fragile. Indeed, everything we know and take for granted as normal reality is revealed to be an artifact, a facade. Behind it lurks an altogether different reality. The state of consciousness that follows from this insight Musil calls "the other condition" (*"der andere Zustand"*) and the search for its attainment is a central theme of Musil's entire opus.

If I were to suggest a single word to describe this insight, the one that would occur to me is the hard-to-translate German word *Doppelbödigkeit.* It derives, I think, from the theatre, and refers to a structure, such as a stage that has more than one floor; those who walk about on the upper floor may at any moment fall through a trapdoor onto the lower one. The insight that Proust and Musil were interested in is that ordinary reality is indeed *doppelbödig.* It pretends to be self-evident, secure, and formidably strong. Really it is none of those things. There is another reality, vastly more powerful, with various entrance points in the world of the ordinary. Once these transition points are glimpsed, life can never be the same. The normal pursuits of social life are not necessarily devalued thereby, but their assumptions can no longer be taken for granted. Even if "the other condition" remains a rare experience in the life of an individual, the memory will remain and ensure that normal living will never again be completely spontaneous.

While this kind of insight may be facilitated by catastrophic events, it does not necessarily depend upon them. It can be had, so to speak, less expensively. To make this point, let me recount a quite trivial incident in my own experience. I was with a friend in a hotel lobby in Honolulu, waiting for some other people to join us for dinner. As we were standing there, a door opened on one side and out came a group of elderly Japanese ladies dressed in kimonos. We hardly paid any attention to them; elderly Japanese ladies, even if dressed in kimonos, are not a rare sight in Honolulu. Then the door opened again, releasing another group of similarly clad elderly Japanese ladies. And again. And again. There appeared to be something of a rhythm: Every twenty seconds or so the door reopened, releasing another group of five or six Japanese ladies. By the time this had happened eight or ten times, and a group of some forty or fifty ladies had congregated in the lobby, my friend and I began to pay attention. At first with mild interest, then with some bemusement—and then with something like dread. The door continued to close and reopen rhythmically (or so it seemed), and more and more elderly Japanese ladies spilled out into the lobby. I turned to my friend and said: "Look, I think we are seeing here a hole in the universe. This is it: There is a hole. And out of it will come an unending number of elderly Japanese ladies in kimonos. They will keep coming. This will never stop." My friend laughed, although somewhat uneasily. We watched nervously as the entire hotel lobby came to filled with these ladies. And then the whole thing stopped. In the end, there were about a hundred ladies in the lobby, and of course there had to be a perfectly ordinary explanation. This was a tour group catering to elderly women, or possibly these were the wives of some Japanese conventioneers. In any case, when the invasion stopped, my friend and I laughed with a sort of relief, joked about the event, and then, as we were joined by our dinner companions, went out. It was a trivial incident, not even good for a story at dinner. Nor was it in any way a frightening experience. And yet, for a few minutes, the reality of ordinary life was put in question.

I hardly need to emphasize that I am not offering this story as an example of religious experience. Even the most eccentric believer is not likely to put his faith in a universe full of an infinity of elderly Japanese ladies (though one might think of much worse possibilities). My point is that ordinary reality can be punctured quite easily and once this has happened, anything is possible. This insight is certainly not the result of an act of belief. It is typically not an act of any kind; not something I did, but something that happened to me. All the same, these ruptures of reality disclose or at least intimate a *transcendent* reality lying beyond. The insight is not faith. But it opens up the possibility.

The term "transcendence" carries a heavy burden of prior definitions, some of them contradictory, and none completely satisfying. "Sacredness" or "holiness" are two words for the phenomenon, "the supernatural" would be another. Rudolf Otto has provided the most useful definition of the phenomenon that lies at the core of religious experience. (I'm referring to his best-known work, entitled *The Idea of the Holy* in English—a very unfortunate translation from the German, where the title was *Das Heilige* (The Holy): One of Otto's principal points is that it is not the *idea*, but the *experience* of this phenomenon that must be understood.) The thing that such experience purports to grasp is, above all, *transcendent* in that it radically differs from ordinary experience. It is, in Otto's words, "totally other" (*totaliter aliter*). It constitutes, to the ordinary mind, an immense mystery (*mysterium tremendum*). It terrifies, yet also exercises a strange and powerful attraction. In its pristine form it is a manifestation of overwhelming power, pre-ethical (it carries no necessary moral implications) and pre-theoretical (any reflection about it will always occur after the event). In the course of history this phenomenon has taken very different forms, been perceived and explained in vastly different ways, and has engendered or legitimated highly discrepant moralities. Otto makes a very good case that the one quality underlying the multitude of such experiences in history is the quality of *otherness*.

Otto's book and most other works that have followed in the phenomenology of religion have concentrated on what Max Weber called the experiences of "religious virtuosi." These are the great figures of religious history—prophets, saints, mystics, and the like. Otto's prime examples of religious experience are the throne vision of Isaiah and the vision of Krishna's universal form in the Bhagavad Gita—by anyone's reckoning "virtuoso performances" of religious genius, in the Hebrew and Hindu traditions respectively. But one ought also to pay very close attention to what Weber (by no means disparagingly) called "the religion of the masses"—that is, the religious experience of ordinary people, who cannot claim these sorts of visitations. This, of course, is especially true because this category includes most of us (it certainly includes me). Most of us have not been visited by gods or angels, we have not had a voice address us from a burning bush or been overwhelmed by enlightenment as we meditated under a bo tree. Depending on the tradition we adhere to, we might have dwelled on these great occurrences with reverence and derived some inner reward for doing so—an identification with the event, an insight coming from it, perhaps even a faint echo of the original experience. These "virtuoso" events thus become our own experience only by virtue of such relatively feeble adumbrations. I do not mean to denigrate these, as it were, second-hand experiences of transcendence. One may well argue that it is the very purpose of any religious tradition to preserve for generations of ordinary people not only the memory of the great founding events, but the possibility of replicating them in a much lower key. Many of us have obtained comfort, insight, and even a modest measure of spiritual transport from participation in the worship of an ordinary congregation of fellow believers. With all due respect to the virtuosi, I have long maintained that those of us who can only play a mediocre violin should pay attention to the intimations of transcendence that can be found in everyday experience. I have elsewhere called these intimations "signals of transcendence."

The intuition of a transcendent reality beyond the empirical world is not the result of an act of faith. It is, precisely, an experience of *reality* defined as something that exists regardless of our wishes; reality authenticates itself. One may recall the famous conversation between Bishop Berkeley and Dr. Johnson, who became increasingly irritated by the philosopher-bishop's idea that no one could disprove the hypothesis that the world only exists in his mind. Dr. Johnson kicked a stone across the road and exclaimed, "Thus I disprove it!" Of course, on the level of philosophical theory, Berkeley was quite right in maintaining that no one could disprove his solipsistic hypothesis; but Dr. Johnson was equally right, because reality has no need to be proven—it proclaims itself by being there, by allowing us to kick it, by kicking back. This self-authenticating character of transcendence is most powerful in the awe-filled experiences of the great virtuosi. Isaiah had no need for an act of faith to accept the terrifying vision of Yahweh's throne, neither did Arjuna need to be convinced of the reality of the *avatar* sprung on him by his divine charioteer. The sense of self-authenticating reality, however, also pertains to lesser, mellower experiences of transcendence. It is precisely the sense of an other *reality*, not necessarilly wished or sought after, that characterizes these experiences in which the fabric of the world appears to be ruptured.

Faith enters on two levels. The first level is what I like to call the problem of the morning after: Even if an angel appeared to me last night, and even if that visitation was the most absolutely real thing that has ever happened to me, things may look very different to me this morning. I get up, I brush my teeth, I have breakfast, I talk to my family, I read the morning paper—and with each of these actions the memory of last night's angel begins to fade, as the power of the everyday asserts itself. Could it be that I was dreaming, that I imagined the whole thing? Faith at this point means *faith in my own experience.* The second level is that act by which I decide (or decide to believe) that the transcendent reality I have perceived is not only *there,* but is there *for me.* Faith here is *faith in the ultimate benignness of the universe.* I think this formulation comes close to Luther's meaning when he defined faith (*fides*) as trust (*fiducia*): I trust that which is beyond this world to mean well by me; in monotheistic terms, I trust God, who is master of this and all possible worlds, not to abandon His creation.

Invariably, human beings not only experience the world but reflect on that experience. But when it comes to the experiences that put man in touch with the tran-

scendent, a distinctive difficulty arises: Reflection occurs by means of language, but language is rooted in
ordinary reality; it is best geared to the practical concerns of everyday life. Consequently, it is notoriously
difficult to put into language any experience that radically transcends ordinary reality. Al-Ghazali, who spent
the most creative part of his life trying to reconcile the
experience of Sufi mysticism with the language of orthodox Islam, had a wonderful phrase to describe his
solution: After going on at length about the ineffability
of mystical experience, he nevertheless affirmed the necessity of reflecting about it by means of reason because, he said, "reason is God's scale on earth." Theology, in the broadest meaning of the term, is the attempt
to place religious experience on the scale of reason, or
at least to formulate it in the language of reason. (Many
theologians, today as in earlier periods of history, are
reluctant to face up to the difficulty. They tend to con-
found their intellectual formulations of faith with the
substance of that which is believed. This is one of several reasons why theological reflection should not be
left to the professional theologians.)

What, then, are plausible possibilities for theology
in the pluralistic situation?

As long as a religious tradition has the character of
being taken for granted, the theological task is relatively
easy. It is an intellectual exposition of what is taken as
knowledge. Strictly speaking, it is based on certitude
rather than faith. The outside observer may, of course,
question the validity of this certitude, but to the individual within that situation the possibility of doubt concerning the foundations of the tradition is a purely theoretical exercise. Compared to modern man, traditional
man lives in a world marked by a high degree of
certainty.

It would be very wrong to think that such people

no longer exist today. They are present in huge numbers in regions not yet fully transformed by modernization. But even in the heartland of modernity, in Europe and North America, there are surprisingly large numbers of people whose mode of existence can quite accurately be described as traditional: They live in firmly taken-for-granted structures of behavior and thought, and they often manage to preserve this manner of living for a long time even as they navigate the complexities of a modern society. One can recognize such people by a peculiar air of calmness, as compared with the nervousness and anxieties of others. One ought not to disparage the worlds of these people and I, for one, no longer have an interest in disturbing them—though in my younger years, as a novice teacher, it seemed like a great thing to instill doubt in innocent minds. But now, as long as traditionalists do not seek to impose their putative certainties on everyone else, I think that they and their worlds should be accorded personal as well as institutional respect. The one thing I would strongly advise against is any effort by modern people to become like them—first, because it is dishonest, and second, because it is futile. Both the dishonesty and the futility are, I think, intrinsic to most modern versions of neo-traditionalism. The neo-traditionalist, in laying claim to certitude, must deny his own experience of uncertainty. And in behaving as if the traditional affirmations are certain, he must constantly repress his knowledge that he could, if he wanted, affirm something quite different. Because of this, neo-traditionalist (or neo-orthodox) theologies are inherently precarious and those who subscribe to them are prone to sudden, violent conversions to other systems of belief.

It may well be that the quest for certainty is a deeply rooted trait of human nature. If, in the course of a lifetime, we attain this or that certitude, we should gratefully accept it as a gift of grace. But we should not feign to certainties that are, in fact, the result of strenuous and never-ending efforts at faith. By and large, the modern quest for certainty has had both intellectually and morally deleterious consequences. They are all, to use again Erich Fromm's apt phrase, "escapes from freedom." Needless to say, this quest has not only taken religious forms. Indeed, most attempts to leap over the uncertainties of modernity have been secular in content. The fanaticism of many of these neo-traditionalist movements is a direct consequence of the dishonesty ("bad faith," in Jean-Paul Sartre's sense) that underlies them. This is caught nicely in the German ditty, freely translatable as "Be my brother—or I will bash your head in."

One important aspect of the psychology of fanaticism is the surrender to authority. If an individual wants to pretend to a certitude that he does not in fact possess, he badly needs an authority that will validate his vulnerable posture. Probably the Church of Rome has best perfected this validation, but less magnificent efforts abound; and very often the object of faith shifts from the transcendent to the authority that purports to represent it. This can take a humanly benign form, as in the quip I once heard from an Anglican friend, "I'm not at all sure that I believe in God, but I know that I believe in the Church of England." But there are also more murderous versions of this faith in authority, by no means left behind in the age of Torquemada. One cannot emphasize too strongly that the most murderous inquisitors of modern times have represented strictly secular belief systems.

There is nevertheless an alternative to the quest for certainty that need not end in a debilitating relativism. It begins with the acceptance of uncertainty; it proceeds

with the above-mentioned faith in one's own experience. Theologically speaking, this is the procedure I
have elsewhere called "induction"—that is, a mode of
reflection that seeks to fit one's own experiences (not
only those that can be called "religious") with the experiences represented and mediated by the traditions.
Let me add that I intend nothing esoteric or greatly original by this term. In Protestantism there is a stream of
thought going back at least to Friedrich Schleiermacher
that has been "inductive" in more or less this sense—
focusing on religious experience rather than religious
ideation as the object of theological reflection, rejecting
the notion that reason must be abandoned before one
enters the realm of faith, and being prepared to examine
both one's experiences and one's own religious training
in the light of the modern empirical disciplines. I
strongly believe that this approach of liberal Protestantism continues to be valid today, despite its inevitable
appearance of tepidness in the eyes of those who desire
fist-pounding assurance. It was this theological stance
that made Protestantism the first religious body in history to apply the cold instruments of modern historical
method to its own sacred scriptures, while continuing
to affirm their salvific power. This enormously coura-
geous move combined faith in one's own experience
with faith in the God who will not abandon those who
trust in Him. In other words, I do not lie to myself about
whatever my reason and my life have shown me; I refuse to believe that God, who is perfect truth, asks me
to deny whatever truths I may have stumbled on, however imperfect. Since God exists, the only truth is that
which will perdure before His face. If, then, I have
found one truth in the scriptures and another in the insights of critical analysis, there *must* be a way to reconcile the two. I can say that I believe this in the fullest
sense, the sense of faith as trust.

For those of us who have not been visited by angels or transmuted by mystical ecstasies, transcendence can only be experienced in second-hand or fairly muted ways. The traditions, through their scriptures and their worship, mediate what a lawyer might call hearsay evidence concerning transcendence; but this second-hand replication of the founding experiences can often correspond in surprising and powerful ways with the experience of the ordinary believer. A good portion of most people's religious experience is probably of this kind, and not for a moment would I suggest that it should be looked down on. On the contrary, one of the most important *raisons d'être* of religious institutions is their capacity to sustain this kind of experience. But just as it is untrue that there is no salvation outside the Church, it is not true that only in the Church can we find the signals of transcendence.

I have long thought that the signals we can find in ordinary, everyday life are of decisive importance: The recurring urge of human beings to find meaningful order in the world, from the overarching edifices constructed by great minds to the assurance that a mother gives her frightened child; the redemptive experiences of play and humor; the ineradicable capacity to hope; the overwhelming conviction that certain deeds of inhumanity merit absolute condemnation, and the contrary conviction as to the absolute goodness of certain actions of humanity; the sometimes searing experience of beauty, be it in nature or the works of man; and many others one could easily enumerate. Each of these, though quite ordinary in many cases and almost never perceived as supernatural, *points toward* a reality that lies beyond the ordinary: The order my mind imposes on the world intends an order that was there before my mind began to work on it. If my game or my joke can temporarily supersede the tragic dimensions of the hu-

man condition, I can envisage the possibility that tragedy is not necessarily the last or most important thing
one can say about that condition. If I can hope even in
the face of death, then I can at least entertain the
thought that death may not be the last word about my
life. And so on.

These experiences clearly do not unambiguously or
compellingly testify to transcendence. Each of them can
be amply explained in secular terms that bracket or exclude transcendence. Order may indeed be the product
of human minds, and nothing else; *out there*, in the end,
may be nothing but meaningless chance or chaos. My
playing and my joking may be useful ways to escape for
a few moments from the tragedy of being a vulnerable
and mortal being, but in the end, the joke may be on
me. I may hope all I want, but all my hopes will finally
be dashed not only by my own death but by the even-
tual destruction of everyone and everything in whom
or in which I have invested hope. To see in these experiences signposts toward transcendence, therefore, is in
itself a decision of faith. There must be no illusion about
this, no maneuver to bring in the hoary proofs for the
existence of God by the back door. But the faith in these
signals is not baseless, nor is it a mental *acte gratuit*. It
takes my own experience seriously and dares to suppose that what this experience intends is not a lie.

Of all the experiences just credited as signals of
transcendence, the one that has intrigued me most is
humor—more precisely, the experience of the comic.
There is something profoundly mysterious and puzzling about the comic, most of all its power to provoke,
for an instant at least, what is suggestively called "redeeming laughter," even in moments of singular terror
or grief. We all know that these emotions will return
once the moment of laughter has passed. But in that

moment, all the fears and sorrows of existence have been banished; in that moment, if you will, my laughter *intends eternity*. The question, I would contend, concerns the epistemological status of this intentionality. Is it an illusion? Or does it predict and even preempt the redemption that is the eternal destiny of all men? I don't see any compelling answer, either way, to this question. One could say that either conclusion demands an act of belief, though only the religious answer constitutes faith in the sense of trust.

Faith in transcendence is thus by no means a necessary act. For those who still live in a traditional world of taken-for-granted gods, no faith is required; these people, as far as they are concerned, *know* the gods. There is probably no way, aside from self-deception, that we who have been branded by the marks of modernity and pluralism can go back to this sort of certitude. Most people in our situation live as best as they can while avoiding metaphysical questions. Modern America, more than any other contemporary society, has developed techniques and clichés that facilitate avoidance of anything that could shatter the standard operating procedures of pragmatic, problem-solving, essentially optimistic living. To be an American is to march through reality in sensible shoes. One might think that death would be the one event that forces even the most doggedly pragmatic person to ask metaphysical questions. Yet even death has been packaged in America so as to suggest something quite ordinary. Evelyn Waugh wrote a great satire on this American way of death in his novel *The Loved One*. But there is also another, more respectable alternative to faith, namely stoicism—the brave acceptance of tragic inevitability, the refusal to indulge in comforting illusions. This option, I think, merits great respect.

The choice is finally between a closed world or a world with windows on transcendence. It goes without saying that the latter is more hopeful. However, this does not make it less reasonable: Hopelessness does not have a superior epistemological status. Indeed, one might say that, philosophically, it is more reasonable to hope than to despair.

Federico García Lorca wrote an essay on *duende*, a hard-to-translate word that can mean a ghost in colloquial Spanish but which also refers to a mysterious impersonal quality attached to certain events or places. It is related to Socrates' "demon" and to African-American "soul," and is more or less a synonym of Rudolf Otto's "numinous" dimension. Lorca recounts an episode when he and some friends went to hear a famous singer of the so-called "deep song" of Andalusia. They were at first very disappointed by her performance. A middle-aged woman, undistinguished in appearance, she gave a thoroughly uninspired rendition of some Flamenco songs. Then, suddenly, everything changed. All the people in the room sensed it. There was an electrifying tension in the air. And everything about the singer was transformed—her voice, her entire performance, even her appearance. She became as beautiful as her singing. And her song touched a reality utterly beyond the drab surroundings of a tavern in one of the poorer sections of the city. The *duende* had entered.

On the other side of a Christian act of belief the world discloses itself as a sacramental world; that is, a world in which the visible reality contains many signs of the invisible presence of God. Christian faith not only affirms that God will not abandon us, but that He has left scattered evidence of that promise in all sorts of places. To put this in slightly irreverent terms, Christian faith asserts that God plays a vast game of hide-and-seek with mankind, but also that He gives more than a few hints as to where He is hiding.

In the aforementioned essay Lorca quotes one Manuel Torres, who wrote somewhere that *"todo lo que tiene sonidos negros tiene duende"*—"all that which holds dark sounds holds *duende*." This world is a very noisy place. The believer acquires a sort of third ear. Amid all the noise of mundane existence, with a bit of straining, he can hear the dark songs of God.

6

The One Who Is Believed

R eality is haunted by that otherness which lurks behind the fragile structures of everyday life. Much of the time the otherness is successfully held at bay, seemingly domesticated or even denied, so that we can go about the business of living. From time to time we catch glimpses of transcendent reality as the business of living is interrupted or put in question for one reason or another. And occasionally, rarely, the other breaks into our world in manifestations of dazzling, overwhelming brilliance. In these hierophanies, as Eliade called them, the other reality momentarily discloses itself in what appear to be clearly perceived figures. Then, or so it seems, men converse with the gods. Usually, however, the contours of this other reality are far from clear. This means that, most often, the category of transcendence is a negative one. It refers to that which is *not* ordinary reality. But to say that transcendence is usually a negative category does not imply it is empty or useless. It refers to a distinctive and at least partly describable experience, and this experience can be profitably reflected upon. But it is hardly a plausible object of faith in itself.

The affirmation of faith in the Nicene Creed includes a long list of specific items. The most important, the defining object of faith, is the one God whose affirmation leads all the rest. Needless to say, this does not suggest a general belief in transcendence, nor even belief in a personal divinity at the center of all transcendent manifestations. He who is affirmed is the God of Abraham, Isaac, and Jacob, the God who led Israel out of Egypt, who spoke by the prophets, and who is the Father of our Lord Jesus Christ. One can't get much more specific than that! Not only does Christian faith affirm that God is *one,* like other monotheisms, but that He is *the* one who disclosed Himself in the events recounted by the Jewish and Christian Scriptures. In many of these events, according to the biblical accounts, He revealed Himself in such powerful immediacy that the question of belief could not arise at all. The problem was not whether one could believe in this God, but rather how one could withstand His presence and follow His often forbidding demands. This, for worse or for better, is not our situation. We do have a problem of belief, and it not only raises the question of why we should believe in God but why we should believe in *this* God. There are others, after all, and today they are made available in an unprecedented way through the religious supermarket of modern pluralism.

Belief in this God has contested with other beliefs through most of the centuries since a wandering band of nomads first encountered Him on the margins of Near Eastern civilization. There were, of course, times and places where their belief was institutionalized as a taken-for-granted world; but even then, because this has always been a "jealous" God, His representatives wrestled mentally and often physically with those of other divinities. Elijah's contestation with the priests of Baal on Mount Carmel is prototypical of a centuries-long struggle by Yahweh's faithful to prevent their absorption into the polymorphous universe of Near Eastern religiosity. Similar struggles continued through most of Christian history, the longest and (sad to say) bloodiest being the struggle with that other monotheism that broke out of Arabia in the seventh century of the Christian era. Among those contestations in Christian history that involved intensive and sustained intellectual effort, I think one can especially point to three after New Testament times—with the Graeco-Roman world, with Islam, and with modernity. I believe we are now on the edge of a fourth weighty contestation, this time with the religious traditions of southern and eastern Asia. As before, this is much more than a debate between bodies of religious theory. The theories themselves are attempts to articulate vast stocks of human experience, including powerful emotions and moral commitments. What is finally at issue are different ways of experiencing reality.

I have elsewhere made the case that, despite the rich variety of human religion, there are two centers from which the most important and distinct religious possibilities have sprung. In shorthand fashion these two centers may be termed Jerusalem and Benares. To be sure, there are a good many other possibilities of reaching out to transcendence, not least of which is the continuing presence of the mythological matrix in every part of the world. But the really interesting alternative is between the two religious streams that originated in western Asia and on the Indian subcontinent, respectively. The three great monotheistic faiths are rooted in the experience of ancient Israel, Hinduism and Buddhism in the other stream of experience—and these two, in themselves immensely rich and variegated universes of religious experience and thought, represent the most important choice before anyone who takes a religiously global view. Arguments can be made for other candidates, such as Confucianism or Zoroastrianism, but these have not really presented themselves as universally available options either in the past or today. Jerusalem and Benares stand out; the city on which the God whom Israel met in the desert consented to put His seal, where Jesus suffered and died and rose from the dead, and from where Muhammad ascended to heaven; and that other city where all the gods descend at dawn into the healing water of the Ganges, and just outside of which the Buddha preached his first sermon announcing release for all suffering beings. The great messages originating from these two cities have met before, and they are meeting today in a new and potentially mind-shaking way as Asia becomes *present* to the West as it has never been before. This presence will grow and it offers an exceedingly promising challenge to those who confess their faith in the words of the historic Christian creeds.

Since World War II there has indeed been a steadily growing interest among Christian theologians in what came to be called "dialogue" with the great religions of

South and East Asia. Institutionally, this dialogue has been fostered both by the Vatican and by the World Council of Churches; but the most interesting contributions have come from individual scholars, mostly in Western countries, but also notably in India and Japan. This is not the place to go into detail. There may be some use, though, in locating my own approach within the spectrum of theological efforts in this area.

Three broad Christian theological positions have been labeled "exclusivism," "inclusivism," and "pluralism." As with all such typologies, there are individual authors who fall between the cracks. But the typology is helpful in distinguishing major orientations. The "exclusivists" continue to insist that Christianity is the only salvific tradition, the repository of God's only direct revelation to mankind. This position need not at all imply contempt or lack of appreciation for non-Christian religions, but it sets narrow limits on whatever Christian theology may incorporate from them. The "exclusivist" attitude, albeit in an unusually extreme form, is well exemplified by Karl Barth, who regarded all religions as expressions of unbelief. Once, when Barth was going on about Hinduism as unbelief, he was asked how he could say this without having met a Hindu; Barth replied *"A priori!"* There is a rather impressive bloody-mindedness in this stance. I must confess a certain admiration for it, especially after encounters with the wimpishness that is so characteristic of the theological milieu today. But to be impressed is a far cry from being persuaded. And while I'm willing to concede Barth's intellectual integrity in his claim to aprioristic certitude, I'm not so sure about his emulators.

Be this as it may, it is the other two positions that are dominant today among both Protestant and Catholic theologians. The "inclusivists" insist that Christianity represents the closest approach to the fullness of religious truth available to human beings; but they are also prepared to acknowledge truth, even revelatory truth, in other religious traditions. Possibly the most respected representative of this position has been the Catholic theologian Karl Rahner, who has had some influence on official Catholic thinking in this area since the Second Vatican Council. Finally, the "pluralists" are willing to go quite far in relativizing the Christian claim to exclusive truth. Probably the most provocative and certainly prolific representative has been John Hick, who has called for a change in Christian thought that would be comparable to the Copernican revolution in astronomy: No longer will Christianity be seen as the single center of the universe, but rather as one of several bodies circling the center which Hick calls, none too helpfully, "the Real."

Let me try and simplify these various positions. The key proposition, defended by very few today but used as a foil by nearly everyone, is the venerable Catholic formula that *extra ecclesiam nulla salus*—"there is no salvation outside the Church" (non-Catholic theologians have substituted "Christ" or "the Christian faith" for "Church" in the formula, but this does not affect its exclusivity). Exclusivists are those who, in the teeth of the relativistic *Zeitgeist*, go on affirming this proposition. "Inclusivists," especially Catholic ones, may actually assent to the statement that there is no salvation outside the Church. But they will define the concept of "Church" much more broadly than has traditionally been the case, so as to include large numbers of people who were never baptized, who are not part of the Christian community, some of whom may never have heard of Christianity. These are the people whom Rahner rather deftly called "anonymous Christians"—that is, people who are Christians without knowing it. But a better way of describing the inclusivist position is to say that it reverses the classical formula to something like *ubi salus ibi ecclesia*—"where there is salvation, there is the church"—and salvation may be found in religious experiences and scriptures far removed from the Judeo-Christian tradition, quite possibly including those rooted in Benares. Finally, the pluralists are unwilling to speak of only one salvation and even less of one Church, however amplified. They would, precisely, "pluralize" both the *salus* and the *ecclesia* in the formula, at which point the latter cannot really be amplified but must simply be abandoned. Christianity is now one among many human attempts to reach out to the ulti- mate reality, with no particular status of revelatory priv- ilege, though pluralists (Hick among them) will readily admit that Christianity will remain their own point of access to the religious quest.

Nobody is very happy at being put in a category that inevitably simplifies one's thinking and puts one in the company of people with whom one disagrees on some points. However, if I'm pushed to the wall and given no way out, I'd have to say that I must count my- self among the inclusivists. This is not because the truth is usually in the middle. Rather, it is because the exclu- sivists claim an access to truth that I must question and the pluralists tend to give up on the truth question al- together (in the sense that they seem to downplay the considerable conflicts between the truth claims of dif- ferent religious traditions). Thus, if I say that I believe in one God who disclosed Himself through the events between Sinai and Pentecost, then I'm implying a claim to a truth that necessarily excludes others—such as the claim that no god can be dismissed from the plenitude of revelations, or that at the center of reality is not a person but a vast void, or that God's revelation came to an absolute and final apex in the Quran. I can, of course, say that I'm not sure about any of these things; I can even speak of hypotheses instead of creedal affirmations. But even if I put it in such lower keys, the fact remains that my belief either implies truth or it means nothing at all; and if it implies truth, it must also imply error. The full-blown pluralist position sidesteps this fact and at the same time trivializes the experiences out of which faith comes.

If I say that I have Christian faith, I'm saying I believe that the core affirmations of Christian tradition are true and reflect reality—or at least that they are closer to truth than other, contradictory affirmations. If I *don't* mean this, then, whatever it is that I'm saying, I'm not articulating a belief—perhaps a vague intuition, an emotional preference, a judgment of taste, but none of these can meaningfully be described by the words "belief" or "faith." If I do affirm truth, then the only warrant for my affirmation of faith must be a correspondence between the Christian tradition and my own experiences of truth and reality. Paul Tillich used the term "correlation" to denote this correspondence, a good term except for its suggestion that what goes on here is primarily an intellectual exercise. And, as I have argued earlier, intellectual reflection is always secondary to experience in the religious phenomenon: First the divine touches us; later we reflect upon it. Perhaps "touching" is the word to use here: I affirm Christianity because I have been touched by its symbols, because the reality it alleges fits with my own experiences of what is real about the world, about the human condition, and about my own life. Reality "touches" me in an immediacy of experience, it strikes me, it even wounds me. I think this meaning was intended in the classical

Protestant formulation that the Gospel "convicts" us; in a much lower key, this is what Alfred Schutz meant by an "*aha* experience": I hear this, what I hear fits with everything else I have experienced as reality, and this correspondence moves me to say "*yes*, this must be what the world is all about!"

Of course, when I say something like this, I continue to be fully aware of my location in space and time. I'm an individual of a specific culture, biography, class, and so on, and I know very well that all these specifications will inevitably affect my sense of reality. Nevertheless, when I say I have experienced something as real, I am implying that this "accent of reality" (as William James put it) supersedes all these relativities of my situation. It is my situation that is relative; the truth, by definition, is not. This conviction of truth must then be my criterion by which I assess the claims of others. To do otherwise is to deny or trivialize my own experience, and by the same token to take the truth claims of others less than seriously. For example, I cannot simultaneously affirm the Nicene Creed and the Muslim affirmation that "there is no god but Allah, and Muhammad is His prophet"—or that at the center of reality is the emptiness of Buddhist enlightenment. I need not propose that there are no truths disclosed in the experiences that underlie these other affirmations. But I must assess them with reference to my own convictions (using the term in its classical Protestant sense). This assessment inevitably subordinates other convictions to my own, but it implies no lack of respect for these other convictions; on the contrary, it takes them with utmost seriousness on their own terms—that is, as claims to truth.

Put simply, if I propose that all religious traditions are equal in their truth contents, I am saying in effect that there is no such thing as truth. I can disguise this conclusion by redefining the word "truth" in such a way as to deprive it of any transcendent reality referent—say, as a symbolization of this or that immanent reality, as has been done by a large number of modern philosophical, psychological, and sociological theories. All these theoretical exercises effectively liquidate the phenomenon they purport to explain; when theologians engage in this type of exercise, they commit a kind of prolonged epistemological suicide—a spectacle that has profoundly comic aspects. But further, if I propose that different religious traditions are *un*equal in their access to truth, I must use my own conviction of truth as the criterion by which I assess the *degree* to which truth may be found in some or all of these traditions. It cannot be emphasized strongly enough that this attitude in no way reflects ethnocentric arrogance or narrowness. It is no more and no less than the necessary consequence of the root religious insight that there is a transcendent *reality* and the empirical acknowledgment of the fact that there are different, even contradictory accounts of this reality. Having said this, however, I can take a further step: I can entertain the thought that those great streams of tradition which embody millennia or centuries of human experience and thought are very unlikely to be nothing but a long story of illusion. Taking this step, of course, immediately embroils me in precisely the sort of comparative assessment of truth claims just indicated.

To *propose,* or *assess*—these are words that refer to theoretical activities of the mind. It is always necessary to recall that religion is not primarily a matter of theorizing about the world: Religious experience always precedes religious reflection. In trying to engage other religious traditions it is quite possible to bypass all theorizing and instead to attempt, as far as I am able, to participate in the experience. This is by no means a use-

less experiment and it can often be successful; it sometimes even leads to the disturbing result that this other
experience touches me in such a way that I'm forced to
revise some, perhaps even all, of my previous religious
convictions.

Thus I can join the pilgrims who flock at dawn toward the river in Benares, immersing themselves in an
infinity of gods, and I too can at least approximate the
experience of a world in which supernatural beings per-
meate every rock, every tree, every drop of water. I can
engage in meditational exercises which, however feebly, replicate the great mystics' experience of the self
fading away, being absorbed in an ocean of divinity, an
endless silence in which there are no selves and no
gods. There is a bo tree in every one of us—or, in the
language of that tradition, each one of us can discover
the Buddha-body within ourselves. I can also join those
who pray in any of the myriad mosques that stretch
from the Atlantic Ocean to the China Sea and, however
inadequately, share in the submission to the blazing
majesty of this one God, who is relentless speech, will,
purpose. I'm certainly capable of suspending all reflection or theorizing as I do these things. I would go further and say that there are occasions on which such sus-
pension of intellectual activity is just what is called for.
But there will be the mornings after. Then reflection is
not just an option but an obligation. Let me recall once
more that wonderful saying of al-Ghazali, that reason is
God's scale on earth: Having received the gift of reason,
I have an obligation to use it. On the morning after, as
I remember my experiences of those other paths toward
transcendent reality, I must recall my previous convictions of truth, I must compare and assess. This will indeed be an act of theorizing, very much in the Tillichian
mode of "correlation."

It is here that I see a very great challenge to Christian thought, and I think it is a good sign that a growing number of theologians are taking up the challenge. As always in such cognitive encounters, the best outcome is not just better understanding of the other but a better understanding of oneself. Obviously there are a very great number of theoretical loci emerging from the confrontation of Christian thought with different non-Christian traditions. I'm not at all sure how to establish priorities here; probably this will depend on the particular situation of the theorizers—Indian Christians, for instance, are likely to have different priorities here than their fellow believers in Japan, or in Africa, or in Western countries. I can only indicate here three loci that have seemed important to me as I have reflected about these matters in recent years, and I do so without any implications of priority or exclusivity: I would propose the need for a Christian theory of *divine plenitude*, a Christian theory of *emptiness*, and a Christian theory of *revelations*. In each case I assume that the theorizing proceeds in fidelity to Christian convictions of truth *and* in the belief that there is truth to be found in other convictions. In other words, I assume an intellectual exercise that is neither self-liquidating nor self-aggrandizing.

Instead of speaking of a Christian theory of divine plenitude, one could just as well speak of a theory of the mythological matrix or even a theory of polytheism. In this context it is vital to abandon, resolutely, any notion of progress—any notion, that is, that such a view of reality is "immature," "obsolete," belonging to "the childhood of the human race." To be sure, there is good evidence that certain historical stages of consciousness are replicated in the development of every individual child. But this evidence should not be confused with the proposition that "we latecomers" or "we adults," as the case may be, have a status of epistemological privilege. It is quite possible that in the dawn of its history the human race had an access to reality that it subsequently lost, as it is possible that this reality is briefly accessible in childhood and then lost in the basically depressing process of growing up. If so, what we commonly think of as progress may actually be a devastating story of epistemological deprivation. Let me for a moment speak as a polytheistic theorist: The gods who once spoke to us have now fallen silent. Perhaps it is because we make so much noise.

The mythological matrix is not just a thing of the past. It is an ever-present possibility of enchantment and reenchantment. Must we say that this is simply an ever-present possibility of illusion? I think not. Of course Christian faith is necessarily, inevitably mono-theistic. The God of Christian faith can only be *one* God, and in Christian experience the entire world points to this all-encompassing oneness. But this does not mean that Christian thought can specify the number of faces that God can assume in order to show Himself to men. The development of Trinitarian doctrine in and of itself testifies to the conviction that God has more than one face, that He is literally more than one "person." There are other, rich resources in the history of Christian thought for a theoretical development in this area— from the Johannine books in the New Testament it-self, through various movements of Christian Neoplato-nism and mystical doctrine, to the conception of the icons in Eastern Christendom. In order to obey the First Commandment one need not denude the universe of every divine manifestation not reported in the biblical canon.

A key proposition might be that Christian faith en-visions *a sacramental universe*. Sacraments, in the classical Christian view, are visible signs of an invisible grace—but signs not only in the sense of an abstract symbol (as the signature on a document symbolizes agreement), but as a living, efficacious presence (as an embrace signifies the presence of affection). In this latter sense the Christian can affirm that the world is full of the signs of God's presence. He will also have to affirm that sometimes there are false signs, or misleading ones. Already in the Hebrew scriptures there is the recurring question of how to distinguish true and false prophecy. The criterion implied there is also relevant to the present problem. It is a criterion of *consistency*: The God who said A cannot also have said B, if B contradicts everything contained in A. Thus, for example, the Hebrew mind found it (probably progressively) inconsistent that the God who revealed Himself to Israel in moral commandments should require human sacrifices. If this God stopped Abraham from sacrificing Isaac, faith in Him will also provide criteria for determining that some alleged manifestations of divine plenitude are indeed false. It follows, for example, that an inclusivist Christian theology will not hesitate to repudiate the widespread Mesoamerican belief that the gods require ongoing human sacrifices; to the extent that this belief was central to that religious worldview, its sacramental quality will be doubtful at best. This does not preclude the possibility, even the likelihood, that other aspects of the (so to speak) Mesoamerican path to transcendence do indeed point toward truth. There are presences that still brood over these abandoned pyramids, deep in the jungle or on lonely, windswept hilltops, and I, for one, would not like to say that they are merely memories of all the human anguish that called out from the sacrificial platforms. Be this as it may, it is not plausible to suggest that the dialogue between the traditions requires a Christian theory of the sacred massacres of the Aztecs. (Luckily, Aztec priests are not around today to participate in conferences for inter-religious dialogue. I hate to imagine how some of our multiculturally sensitive "pluralists" would deal with them! Though it is not irrelevant to recall that the same sensitive types were earnestly engaged in dialogue with Marxism while more human beings were sacrificed in the name of *that* god than died in all the centuries of the Mesoamerican blood cults.)

Bonaventure, who employed Neoplatonist categories to account for the Franciscan experience within the boundaries of Catholic orthodoxy, spoke of God as the *fontalis plenitudo*, the fountain-plenitude of all the wonders of the world which Francis had embraced in his mystical ecstasies. It is an attractive phrase, not just in its poetic allusion, but in opening up avenues of theoretical reflection. Such reflection is of particular value in the modern situation. For more than a century and a half, modern theories of religion have been mesmerized by Ludwig Feuerbach's concept of religion as a projection of human ("anthropological") concerns, symbolizing not some transcendental reality but the very mundane realities of human existence. Not only did Marx, Nietzsche, Freud, and Durkheim construct their theories of religion on this Feuerbachian foundation; much of recent Christian theology has been an effort to build on the same base. It is important to acknowledge that the Feuerbachian agenda of converting theology into anthropology is feasible and, up to a point, valid. Religious ideas and institutions do indeed reflect a multitude of social and psychic concerns, including most of those explored by the aforementioned authors. But so do ideas and institutions of, for example, modern science. Thus a demonstration that Einstein's theory of rel-

ativity was a projection of the social and intellectual relativism of early twentieth-century Germany does not
excuse us from asking whether this theory helps us understand the movements of the galaxies. To reduce astronomy to sociology or psychology will impress anyone as a ludicrous enterprise; the same reduction
applied to theology only seems less ludicrous to those
who have already given up on the idea that there may
be a transcendent reality. The fact that many contemporary Christian theologians have done just that will be
a source of mirth to future intellectual historians.

A Christian theory of divine plenitude will (to bor-
row a famous Marxian formulation) stand Feuerbach on
his head: The symbolized turns out to be the symbol.
Modern thought has interpreted religion as an aggregate of symbols, that which is symbolized being the empirical world, especially the world of human beings. To
propose a sacramental view of the universe is to invert
the Feuerbachian view (without denying its utility in
understanding certain empirical connections). It is the
empirical world in its entirety which now comes into
view as a gigantic symbol. That which it symbolizes, in
countless broken images, is the blazing reality that lurks
behind this world—in Christian terms, the face of God.

To propose the need for a Christian theory of emptiness is to refer in particular to the confrontation with
Buddhism, especially its Mahayana traditions, with
their rich body of highly sophisticated reflection about
the experience of nothingness (*nirvana*) or emptiness
(*shunyata*). There is good warrant for this, because it can
be argued that this confrontation is likely to bear the
richest fruits for Christian theology. But one could more
generally speak of a theory comprehending all forms of
the so-called "mysticism of infinity," in which the individual experiences a fading away of both self and

world, followed by a merging with what is perceived as the absolute reality, characterized simultaneously by total annihilation and total bliss. Most Buddhist traditions understand this experience as the validation of the doctrine of non-self (*an-atta* in the Pali canon), which asserts that the self is ultimately an illusion. What appears to be the same experience, however, has been interpreted in quite different ways by other traditions, as in the Upanishadic doctrine of the ultimate identity of *brahman* and *atman*, that is, of the core reality of the universe and the core reality of the self. This Hindu version of a seemingly cross-cultural experience has been classically caught in the formula *"tat tvam asi"—you* [the true self] are *that* [the divine reality at the center of all reality]. In much less reflected-upon versions the experience can be found in all religious traditions, virtually all over the world, in which the transcendent is approached by way of ecstatic practice.

For obvious reasons this experience has been most difficult to interpret in the context of the three great monotheistic traditions: How can one assert unity with the awesome God who revealed Himself as the all-powerful person, speaking, acting, with specific purposes in the destinies of men? Not all mysticism is of the type called *advaita* (non-dualistic) in Hinduism, where self and divinity are united in the ecstatic experience. Franciscan mysticism is one example of a quite different experience in which the duality of self and divinity is clearly maintained. But whenever Jewish, Christian, or Muslim mystics came close to the "infinity" experience, they always tottered on the edge of heterodoxy, sometimes falling right over it, and often enough they got into unpleasant difficulties with their respective religious authorities. Thus the daring mystical speculation of the Safad school of the Kabbalah was highly suspect to the rabbinical guardians of Jewish tradition; Meister Eckhart's teachings were condemned by the Church (luckily for him, after his death); and almost all the Sufis collided with the official representatives of Muslim orthodoxy. A paradigmatic case was that of al-Hallaj, who ran in ecstasy through the streets of Basra shouting *"ana'l-hagg."* The Arabic words literally mean "I am the truth"; the religious authorities, probably correctly, understood his meaning to be "I am God," and executed al-Hallaj for blasphemy.

The more prudent mystics refrained from too much theorizing about their experiences and thus kept out of trouble. Where they did theorize, they often employed some version of the Neoplatonist concept of divine emanations. Isaac Luria and his disciples in Safad developed the doctrine of *tsimtsum,* or contraction, according to which God contracted His all-pervasive being, leaving a void so that the act of creation could bring forth the universe. The mystical experience transports the individual back into that void, a timeless moment that awaits the divine speech by which the world was created. According to Gershom Scholem, the doctrine served to protect this school of Jewish mystics from falling into a pantheism that would have propelled it beyond the boundaries of Judaism. Very similar ideas can be found in Sufism, as in the writings of al-Tustari (I owe this example to Gerhard Böwering) where the mystical experience is interpreted as a return to the primeval moment before the creation of the world, the so-called "day of the covenant," when all yet-to-be-created souls were summoned to affirm their allegiance to God. All these speculations are intended to reconcile faith in the personal God with the experience of impersonal divinity; they establish a hierarchy of meanings in which the personal finally subordinates the impersonal. Interestingly enough, there are similar theories in theistic Hinduism (as in Ramanuja's interpretations of *bhakti* devotion) and in some schools of Pure Land Buddhism. In the latter the problem is how to reconcile devotion to the Bodhisattvas, the very personal savior figures, with the utterly trans-personal experience of enlightenment.

At the heart of Christian faith is the God who addresses man. In the biblical records this spans Yahweh's thunderous speech on Sinai and the Johannine *logos*, the word which antecedes creation and which became incarnate in Christ. The "mysticism of infinity" experiences, not divine speech, but a vast silence. Christian reflection will have to order these meanings in such a way as to subordinate God's silence to God's address. The void of mystical experience can then be understood as the silence that waits for God's speech, an emptiness which is blissful precisely because it will be filled with the plenitude of God's immeasurably creative power.

One of the classical Mahayana texts, *The Holy Teaching of Vimalakirti* (translated by Robert Thurman) opens with a convention of thirty-two thousand Bodhisattvas debating various aspects of what Vimalakirti calls the "inconceivable liberation." Each one represents a "Buddha-field," a cosmos within which his particular power of redemptive compassion is at work to liberate sentient beings from suffering and death. Can we imagine the apostle Peter visiting this congress and repeating there his sermon reported in the fourth chapter of the Book of Acts, which ends with the lapidary sentence, "And there is salvation in no one else, for there is no other name under heaven given among men by which we must be saved?" Must we take Peter at his word and relegate that entire world of striving for redemption to the realm of illusion or idolatry? Or is it possible that, hidden somewhere in this conclave of redeemers, we could come on the presence of him whom Peter met with such shattering impact on the shore of Lake Galilee? I am reminded here of a poem by Hölderlin invoking the gods of Greece who fascinated him so much. After tracing the footsteps of these luminous figures across the landscape of the classical Mediterranean world, the poet confesses that, in all this glory, he misses the one with whom he had fallen in love long ago—in his childhood, we may presume, in the vastly different physical and spiritual landscape of Swabian pietism. How can a German Lutheran cope with Apollo? Is there a bridge from Galilee to the awesome Himalayas of Indian soteriology?

When I suggest a Christian theory of revelations, I have something different in mind from the previously discussed issue of the divine plenitude. What concerned me before was that mythological matrix which antedates all gods and saviors. What concerns me here are those ruptures of the mythological matrix, outside the Judeo-Christian stream of revelation, where other figures of redemption were perceived by men. Inevitably, Christian faith has been focused on this one figure of Jesus, in whose life, death, and resurrection, Christians believe, the redeeming love of God has been revealed once and for all. Inevitably too, in the dazzling brightness of this revelation no other redeeming figure, "no other name," was conceivable. But we are not the apostles. We are much farther from this event, and I am not persuaded that their perceptions must be absolutely binding on us. To put it bluntly, it is possible that Peter was exaggerating a bit. What is more, Christian thought ever since those early days has tried to grapple with a perception of Christ's action in the world that transcends the brief lifespan of Jesus of Nazareth—already in the New Testament in the Johannine doctrine of the *logos*, in the development of ideas concerning the Holy

Spirit and the Trinity, in the Christological cosmologies of the Church Fathers. These are all theories, but what underlies them is the experience of a redeeming power at work in the world at different times and in different places, a power that Christians must necessarily identify with the name of Jesus Christ. It was this same perception that led Christianity to, as it were, annex the entire religious history of Israel. Yet given the perspective of Christian faith, this appropriation was inevitable—however much we may today rightly try to mitigate its offensiveness to Judaism. It seems to me that our present question must be whether a comparable theoretical procedure is called for in dealing with the other great world religions.

There have been a number of such attempts in recent years. The work of John Hick may be cited again here. Raymond Panikkar has tried something similar in many books—first in his *The Unknown Christ of Hinduism*, where he gives a Christological commentary on the figure of Ishvara, the creator-god in various Hindu traditions. Kenneth Cragg, best known for his interpretations of Islam, has recently suggested (in *The Christ and the Faiths*) that we might look on the biblical canon as "a Mediterranean source book . . . for a world theology"; the suggestion is that there are other sources, outside the Judeo-Christian stream. I do not mean to disparage these efforts, some of them admirably bold, when I say that they only represent first steps in this direction. I am also well aware of the dangers of an incautious syncretism (not to say a wimpish sentimentality) in this sort of enterprise. Nevertheless, I think that here is an immense challenge which Christian theology will have to meet in the years to come.

To be a Christian means to have been arrested by this one face to such an extent that there had to be the affirmation that God was reflected in it. Having caught a glimpse of that face, one will go on looking for it. Federico García Lorca, in his "Poem of the Saeta," speaks of the brown Christ (*Cristo moreno*) and sees him pass "from the lily of Judea to the carnation of Spain," a procession in which this face takes on new colors and new shapes. We may look for it yet elsewhere. If God was in Christ, then He must be wherever redeeming power is transforming reality. This cosmic Christ, savior of this and all possible worlds (including the "inconceivable" worlds of the Indian religious imagination), is everywhere, eternally. This is what was affirmed in the prologue to the Gospel of John, whose doctrine of the *logos* annexed, as it were, the entire universe of Hellenic experience: "He was in the beginning with God; all things were made through him, and without him was not anything made that was made." In other words, there are no limits to the *logos*, to Christ, in either time or space: He is present in all reality.

Part III

The Consequences
of Believing

7

The Problem of Ecclesial Belonging

If one takes a religious stance along the lines indicated in the preceding chapters, where does one belong in the bewildering array of Christian churches, communities, and movements on the contemporary scene? Does one have to belong to a church at all? Must this sort of faith express itself in a community? The last question was the most important one, and we can try to answer it sociologically or theologically. Sociologically, for reasons about to be elucidated, the answer must be clearly affirmative. Theologically, I think, the matter is more complicated.

Sociologically speaking, the relation between religious experience and religious institutions is ambiguous. On the one hand, religious experience would remain a highly fugitive phenomenon if it were not preserved in an institution; only the institutionalization of religion allows its transmission from one generation to another. On the other hand, it can be argued that one of the central functions of religious institutions is to domesticate, to render harmless, and thus to distort the experience that serves as their ostensible basis. The institutional imperative, of course, is a fact of human existence that is by no means restricted to religion. Nothing human survives except in an institutional form. This proposition employs the concept of institution in its conventional sociological sense—as a *patterning* of human activity and thought that can be shared within a particular group of people. Such patterning allows us to recognize each others' intentions, to find a common ground for projects of every sort, and to initiate every new cohort of children into a common universe of discourse. If it were not for institutions, every human encounter would be totally new and unpredictable, as if Adam encountered Eve all over again in the dawn of time. Institutions, as Arnold Gehlen put it, "unburden" us—that is, they relieve us of having to reinvent the social order and indeed the world itself every time we interact with other human beings. What is more, as especially Maurice Halbwachs has shown, we could remember very little even of our own experience if we could not place it in a social frame of reference—which inevitably means an institutional frame of reference. Men are profoundly social beings. And this means that their existence must unfold within some sort of institutional order.

Let me return for a moment to what earlier I called the problem of the morning after—the problem of how to make sense of experiences of transcendence in their immediate aftermath. I strongly suspect that even the greatest virtuosi of religious experience had this problem. Thus Paul, having encountered the risen Christ on the road to Damascus, found refuge in the Christian community in that city and it was there, we may surmise, that he began to make sense of the utterly shocking event. Thus Muhammad, after the angel addressed him on Mount Hira, according to one tradition was terrified beyond words, ran in panic to his home, and asked his wife to hide him so that the angel would not find him again—and it was in conversation with that understanding and deeply religious woman, we might surmise, that he began to reflect upon his own experience. A sociologist might say that the first Muslim community consisted solely of Muhammad and Khadijah, who, if there were such a title, would have to be called the mother of Islam. And thus too we find, over and over again, that mystics, having informed us that their experience is completely beyond verbal description, tell us what happened in language derived from their particular religious tradition, thus, in a strict sense, *institutionalizing* the experience. Teresa of Avila, in her ecstasies, believed she had seen Jesus; it does not require a great act of the imagination to think that had she lived in India, she would have given a different name to the transcendent being with whom she was confronted.

What is true of the virtuosi is even truer of the masses—the rest of us, the *hoi polloi* of the religious enterprise, who encounter transcendence most of the time (if at all) in an institutional setting of worship and instruction. No miracles for us, no angels, no transfigurations; just a glimmering of transcendence in a transitory and usually solitary experience of wonder, a remembered sunset or a redeeming smile, or a long ago moment in church, or a passage in something once read. Needless to say, such experiences are much more fugitive and effervescent than the mighty visitations experienced by a Paul or a Teresa. To make sense of them, literally to be able to remember them, we require a frame of reference that typically derives from the institutionalized tradition in which we are rooted (by birth or a later event). Religious institutions function precisely to make a tradition *available* in this manner. As far as the founding experience or message is concerned, the institution makes it possible for these to be retrieved by ordinary people, often removed by many generations from the originating events. Thus one can say that religious experience is represented in an institution in the useful double meaning of this word: The institution symbolizes the experience and also *re-presents* it, in the sense of making available in the present an event that first occurred long ago. Without religious institutions even the experiences of the greatest prophets or mystics would be lost when they disappeared from the earth. Actually, without religious institutions there would be no history of religion.

Furthermore, religious institutions are necessary to provide a plausibility structure for religious beliefs. In this, once more, religion is not unique; every belief requires such social support. One can only say that religion is particularly in need of it because of the extraordinary and (for most people) meta-empirical character of its affirmations. I require social support for what I believe about my fellow men, despite the fact that I deal with them every day; without such support, trust would have to be reestablished time and again, in every human interaction. But I have never seen the gods; if I am to affirm my belief in them, I very much need social support for this belief. The sociologist can, therefore, allow himself a somewhat disrespectful translation of the aforementioned adage that there is "no salvation outside the church," to wit: "No plausibility without the appropriate plausibility structure." This is true of anything that human beings find plausible; it is true of religious beliefs *a fortiori*. In that perspective, the Church is simply the place where Christians huddle together and assure each other that they are right, while all the others—Greeks, Jews, Muslims, or agnostics—are in error.

But religious institutions not only preserve, hand on, and make plausible a particular religious experience; they also, as it were, domesticate it. At the heart of religious experience, as we have said, is the extraordinary, that other which shatters the taken-for-granted certitudes of everyday life. If this kind of experience were allowed to be indulged in at any time and place, ordinary living would become impossible. In other words, religion is a clear and ever-present danger to social order. The purpose of religious institutions, in that perspective, is to contain this danger. No longer can prophets or mystics roam around freely; the institution confines them to specific times and places, and religious experience now becomes safely *scheduled* and *segregated*. Only in this form can it co-exist with and even serve to legitimate ordinary social life. Max Weber, in his celebrated theory of charisma, understood this process of domestication very well. He had a good word for it—in German, *Veralltäglichung*; literally, making something into an everyday occurrence—translated quite sensibly into English as "routinization": That which transgresses all the boundaries of everyday reality is pressed back into the latter's confine; that which was utterly different from anything that ever happened before (or so it seemed) has now itself become a routine occurrence. Religious institutions perform this trick routinely indeed. The original religious event was astounding and profoundly threatening, as the New Testament repeatedly reports the reaction of those who heard Jesus preach: They were astounded, amazed, apparently greatly troubled. The Greek word is *thaumazein*, denoting the reaction to a magical or miraculous event. But, generations later, a Christian can read those astounding words in his Bible or hear them pronounced in church and feel, at most, a twinge of excitement—one that is perhaps unsettling for a moment, but which can readily be reintegrated into the habits and mindset of ordinary, everyday living. The Church makes sure that nothing "worse" happens.

A good illustration of this process comes from biblical scholarship concerning prophecy in the ancient Near East. There are different views of this, especially as regards prophecy in Israel, but there is a strong body of opinion that understands the phenomenon in institutional terms. The biblical term "schools of prophets" would seem to refer to such an institution—prophets (that is, individuals who spoke with the voice of a god) attached to a sanctuary under the control of priests. One can imagine the process that led to this institutional solution. Imagine that, originally, prophets roamed freely all over the place. They would appear at all times and in different locations, even in sanctuaries, and shriek out their messages of divine instruction, often if not always accompanied by the spasms of possession. A most disturbing situation. Priests are in the business of managing disturbances. Who knows what priestly genius first invented what in retrospect appears as the obvious solution: Since we cannot get rid of these characters, let us put them on the payroll. We'll allow them to do their thing on Tuesdays and Thursdays, from noon till sundown, and we'll restrict them to the courtyard in front of the sanctuary's side entrance; this way we'll be able to keep an eye on them. And perhaps we can even charge admission. This operation has been successfully performed by sundry priesthoods ever since.

One can further distinguish "strong" and "weak" institutions. No value judgment is implied with this distinction; it is simply descriptive. A strong institution is one whose patterns of behavior and of thought have been internalized to the point of being taken for granted, seemingly self-evident, and therefore not in need of much reflection. A sociologist might say that such an institution does adequately what institutions are supposed to do, namely to relieve individuals of the burden of making too many decisions. People who live in such an institutional context can afford to act "spontaneously," and they are unlikely to be afflicted with self-doubt or uncertainty. By contrast, a weak institution, while it continues to pattern or "program" behavior, does so much less reliably. The degree of internalization is more superficial, the taken-for-granted patterns are more easily shattered, all sorts of questions come to mind. In consequence, individuals are pushed into reflection and uncertainty. Of course, there is a continuum of "strong" and "weak" institutions, but as one approaches either pole the difference becomes sharply visible.

This difference can be clarified by means of an old American joke. Two friends meet on the street in southern California. One looks very unhappy, and the other asks him why. "I now have a job. A terrible job." "What's so terrible about it?" "Well, let me tell you what I have to do. I work in an orange grove. All day long I sit in the shade, under a tree, and these other guys bring me oranges. I put the big ones in one basket, the little ones in a second basket, and the in-between ones in a third basket. And that's what I do all day long." His friend says, "I don't understand. This seems to me like a very pleasant job. What bothers you about it?" To which the first replies, *"All those decisions!"*

These institutional distinctions are particularly relevant to an understanding of modernization. One important feature of this process is a paradox: While some institutions are greatly strengthened, others are very much weakened. The large structures of a modern economy and state are "strong" institutions indeed. They appear to those who live in (or under) them as immensely powerful, acting by a logic of their own which is hard to resist and often even hard to understand. This characteristic of modern institutions is what Marx had in mind with his concepts of "reification" and "alienation": Such institutions appear as powers independent of the will and the actions of the people who comprise them; consequently these human beings feel helpless and abandoned in their grip. (Marx was wrong in ascribing this characteristic to *capitalism* whereas it really appertains to the much wider category of *modernity*. It has become amply clear that socialist institutions, which are a non-capitalist form of modernity, are much more "reified" and "alienating" than anything Marx criticized.) But at the same time other institutions are greatly weakened. This is generally true of all institutions that are not parts of the economic and political mega-structures, such as those that govern private life or those (to use a term that has lately become popular again) that belong to "civil society"—the family, patterns of sexuality and interpersonal relations, education, aesthetic canons, and religion. In these spheres there has been a process that Arnold Gehlen described (probably with some exaggeration) as "de-institutionalization", with the important implication that individuals must now reflect and make decisions on how to organize these areas of living. As I have argued earlier, pluralism is an important (though not the only) factor in bringing about "weak" institutions.

Gehlen also understood that this situation is not an easy one for individuals. It burdens them with too many decisions. It brings about a widespread condition of what sociologists call *anomie* or normlessness—a condition in which individuals are deprived of strong social ties and clear rules of conduct. Gehlen also had a term for the solution we achieve in this distressing situation—"secondary institutions"—which are relatively weak institutions designed to cope with areas of life previously dominated by strong ones. One could render Gehlen's term in more colloquial language by speaking of "do-it-yourself institutions." For example: Through most of human history child-rearing was firmly patterned within the institutional context of the family (or more broadly, of kinship), in itself probably the most ancient and for centuries the "strongest" institution. This meant, quite simply, that when a child was born the adults in charge knew exactly what to do. Whether what they did was good or bad for the child need not concern us here. The point is simply that there was no uncertainty, no need for reflection or choice. Not so today, in highly modernized social contexts. A child is born and hardly anybody knows what to do. The parents typically do not. There are their mothers who, if old enough to have come from a less modernized situation, may have very firm ideas on the subject. But these ideas are suspect precisely because they come from a less modern, therefore less "enlightened" source. The new parents may turn to members of their own generation who have had children, but the advice they get is likely to be diverse and contradictory. Given these difficulties, very brave parents may decide to really "do it themselves," reinventing child-rearing from scratch using whatever inspiration is handy. Most modern parents are not that brave (or just too busy). What then? Lo and behold, there is a "secondary institution" at hand, ready to help. It can be called, broadly speaking, the child-rearing industry. It consists (especially in America) of a vast network of public and private agencies as well as alleged professionals individually operating clinics, referral services, day-care facilities, nursery schools, counselors and therapists of every description, and full-time givers of advice, in print and in the media. In that respect, for many years, Dr. Benjamin Spock was an institution all by himself, probably commanding more authority than the pope.

But this returns us to our major theme of pluralism: What distinguishes these secondary institutions from their predecessors is that there are many of them. Indeed, in capitalist societies they compete with each other in a market; even in the non-market sectors of a modern society, though, especially in the agencies of the welfare state, different coteries of experts and advice-givers compete for the favor of the bureaucracy and a slice of the tax dollar. Thus our new parents have a choice—breast-feeding versus bottle-feeding programs, demand-feeding versus schedule-feeding, lots of hugging and attention for the baby as against training it to be by itself, emphasizing or de-emphasizing "gender identity"—and so on. True to the intrinsic logic of pluralism, individuals must decide between different "denominations" of child-rearing lore. These denominations are indeed institutions; but they are relatively weak ones.

Religion has very clearly been affected by this process of "de-institutionalization," for all the reasons discussed early on in this book. The term "denomination" offers an excellent clue as to what happened. It is, as far as I know, of American origin. As H. Richard Niebuhr argued in his classic work, *The Social Sources of Denominationalism,* the term refers to what is perhaps the key phenomenon of religion in American history—the phenomenon of pluralism. Niebuhr defines a denomination as a church that has come to accept not only the *de facto* existence but the legitimacy of other churches. This acceptance has not come easily to most of the religious groups that settled in this country, but all were forced, sooner or later, to come to terms with the reality of denominationalism. For most of them, needless to say, this was not the result of some moral conversion to tolerance. Rather, it was the force of circumstance that led to this—already in colonial times, the sheer diversity of the settler population—then, with the coming of the Constitution, the force of law added to the force of circumstance. But as we have seen, this tolerance exacts a high price on the level of religious consciousness. On the institutional level, religion becomes "voluntary" and "privatized." No longer is adherence to a particular religious community the taken-for-granted result of an accident of birth. The individual now chooses to adhere, and even if he adheres to the community into which he was born (still the most common case), he knows that this too is a matter of choice. What is more, as a result of secularization, religion has been driven out, almost completely, from the strong institutions of the economy and state. It now becomes a matter of private life—exactly, as we have seen, the area of the highest "de-institutionalization."

Denominationalism, as here understood, has an ambiguous consequence for the problem of ecclesial belonging. Put simply, it makes this a less desperate affair. This result is ambiguous because one can easily find reasons both to deplore and to be grateful for it. Obviously, one reason why belonging to this church or that today is less desperate a decision is because religious convictions have tended to become more superficial in the transition from "confession" to "preference." An individual is unlikely to risk "house, goods, fame, child, or spouse" (in Luther's words) for what has become one opinion among others. In strictly religious terms, this can be seen as an impoverishment, a trivialization. But one may find it difficult to feel nostalgia for an age (such as Luther's) in which religious differences were negotiated by means of the sword, the torture chamber, and the stake. It is regrettably true that people with unshakable convictions are inclined toward these robust instruments of persuasion. By contrast, the author and the readers of this book who live in democracies can consider their religious options, including the question of church affiliation, in a mood of considerable tranquility and in the near-certainty that they will comfortably survive whatever conclusion they arrive at, precisely because they find themselves in the pluralist societies of the democratic West. There are other societies today where this (dare we call it?) trivialization of religion is prevented quite robustly; but I, for one, prefer to live with triviality instead.

There are costs to this social achievement, however, and one cost is the previously mentioned difficulty of living in uncertainty. Denominationalism has created an etiquette of considerable insipidness, beautifully captured in the title of John Murray Cuddihy's insightful book about the contemporary American religious scene—*No Offense*. It is the theological equivalent of asking someone's pardon for living. The threshold of outrage, even at the most extravagant imbecilities, keeps on rising. Everything and anything is seriously dis-

cussed in academia as much as in the popular media. It
is not surprising that some individuals, after cheerfully
moving around in this morass of relativities, find this or
that fanaticism an attractive alternative. It seems to me
one of the great challenges of the pluralist situation to
find a way of religious existence that rejects both these
alternatives.

Arguably the condition of Christian churches is different elsewhere, particularly in Third World countries
where Christians are in the minority. In America, at
least from the viewpoint adopted here, the situation is
hardly inspiring. The question can be rather simply
posed: Where can an individual go whose religious position is liberal (not in a political sense, but in that of a
long-standing liberal Protestant tradition), but who is
nevertheless unwilling to go along with the various secular and secularizing agendas into which so much of
Protestantism has fallen?

Such an individual, sociologically speaking, falls
between two chairs. There is on the one hand the
sprawling world of what is still, somewhat inaccurately,
called "mainline Protestantism"; on the other is the still
vital and indeed burgeoning world of the Evangelicals.
Given the aforementioned theological bias, neither offers much attraction. The "natural" location of such an
individual would of course be somewhere in the mainline. Sociologically speaking, this includes the Episcopalian and Lutheran denominations, despite the fact
that sizable groups within these denominations (which
are, respectively, the Anglo-Catholics and the Missouri
Synod) are uncomfortable with this location. But this
world of mainline Protestantism has been secularized to
such a degree that the word "Church" has a purely historical meaning for many groupings in this milieu
which are in fact voluntary associations for the promo-

tion of various political and psychotherapeutic causes. To be sure, one must make an important distinction between the denominational or interdenominational organizations and local congregations, many of which pay little attention to the manifestos and programs that preoccupy the people at national headquarters. If one only looked at what these people produce, allegedly in the name of the entire membership of their respective constituencies, one would have to conclude that this world is not only totally politicized, but politicized in a narrowly doctrinaire manner. One could paraphrase the old quip by describing it as the leftmost wing of the Democratic party gathered for prayer, except that it is rather unclear what "prayer" means in this context. At the same time, one can drop into many churches supposedly affiliated with these national organizations, participate in a Sunday morning service, and encounter little or nothing of the agendas propounded by headquarters; indeed, some of the people in the pews have, mercifully, never heard of these agendas. Clearly the option remains of finding such a local church and either resisting or shutting out of one's mind the propaganda of the larger organization. Such an option can be called "parochial," in the literal and non-pejorative meaning of the word. It may be assumed that there are large numbers of American Protestants who have taken this course. But there are two problems here. First, in many locales, it may be very difficult to find such a church. Second, even if one is successful, this option entails a kind of "inner emigration" from the larger religious scene that one may find either theologically or personally uncomfortable.

If the mainline scene presents a picture of decline and debility, the Evangelical world at first presents a picture of exuberant health. Here there is still a spirit of

conviction and self-confidence, the forces of secularization are mainly kept outside, and the newcomer is
embraced with warmth and enthusiasm. It is quite possible that this initial picture of health is somewhat de-
ceptive. There are indications (as in the research by
James Hunter) that "cognitive contamination" is at
work here too. But the principal problem for individual
believers is religious and theological. Of course, compared with "inner emigration," it would be very nice
to feel part of a vigorously religious, unambiguously
Christian community. This good feeling would no
doubt be enhanced by the knowledge that, unlike
"mainline" Protestantism, Evangelicalism is a worldwide movement of immense success, indeed *the* most
successful movement of a religious nature today. But
the religious and theological obstacles are formidable.
Not only would one have to assent to a long list of hard-
to-swallow propositions, from the nature of the biblical
texts to the details of the life of Jesus; one would also
have to participate in a religious life of a very distinctive
style, with variations ranging from Pentecostal ecstasies
to the somewhat mellower emotionalism of, say, a
Southern Baptist prayer breakfast. For a liberal Protestant, alas, to be "born again" as an Evangelical is not an
easy project. Being asked to believe and do what Evangelical orthodoxy prescribes may appear the lesser evil
to some who have been made to flee from congregations in which every form of speech other than feminist
English is grounds for aggressive harassment, where
sermons are political harangues and "prayers" the re-
cital of political platforms, and where congregational
life is a symbiosis of activism and group therapy. The
evidence nonetheless suggests that there are not too
many theological liberals who have so chosen. The
more plausible course is to remain unaffiliated.

What has been described here, including the very word "options," implies a consumer market in religious institutions. This observation has been made before by observers of the American religious scene (including myself) whose views have usually been registered with an undertone of condemnation. And, to be sure, there is a superficiality here that offends religious sensibilities. But is this attitude of picking and choosing, of opting in and out of particular churches, of "inner emigration" or of dropping out altogether—is this attitude really so reprehensible? Let us return to the theological question raised earlier: Must Christian faith express itself in community? And if so, in *which* community?

The very great majority of Christians over the centuries would have answered the first question with a thunderous "yes!" With the exception of a few eccentric heretics, Christian history presents us with a near-unanimity on this subject. But when one asks the second question, this unanimity dissolves into a chorus of contradictory and often murderous claims. The longest, loudest, and arguably most murderous has been, of course, the claim of the Roman Catholic church. Centuries of institutional history inevitably add a patina of plausibility to even the most outrageous assertions, and the Roman claim is not all that outrageous. Not surprisingly there have been individuals since the Reformation who have fled Protestant turbulence for what appeared to them the tranquil authority of Rome. Unfortunately, this course also requires a number of intellectual and behavioral sacrifices that few liberal Protestants are prepared to make. The behavioral adjustments, at least for lay people and especially since the relaxing of discipline after Vatican II, are probably less onerous than the ones required by Evangelicalism. Rome, after all, can plausibly present itself as a civilization in addition to being an ecclesial community, and its baroque splendors have little competition to fear from, say, a Southern Baptist subculture. The required sacrifices of the intellect are considerable. Precisely because of its sophistication Rome has been very adept at accommodating different viewpoints, as long as one thing was absolutely clear— the acknowledgment of its own authority. Roman Catholicism stands and falls with this claim to authority. But to acknowledge it requires an enormous act of counter-empirical faith about the intentions and actions of Jesus with regard to the future of his movement, the role of Peter and the early bishops of Rome, and most importantly, God's way of acting in human reality.

If one applies reasonable historical scholarship to the origins of Christianity, the empirical assumptions on which the Roman claim to authority rests are, at best, very questionable. Few if any theologically uncommitted historians would conclude from the available evidence that Jesus intended to form an organization remotely similar to what became the early Church—let alone that he bestowed a particular authority on Peter, instituted particular sacraments, or issued the commission to convert the whole world. As to the status of the bishop of Rome in that dawn of Christian history, it too is much disputed—though it is unclear what a generally accepted primacy would prove other than the dominance of the metropolitan center of the Roman Empire. But a theological stance of the sort I tried to outline in earlier chapters will not easily accommodate the notion that God acts in history exclusively or even primarily through an organization that can be defined in juridical terms. To believe *this* (as indeed to accept what Evangelicals would have us believe) one must believe in a divine revelation that is much clearer, less ambiguous, than the hesitant intimations most of us have been granted. To be sure, just as an act of faith is required to believe in the Christian God, it is possible to make an act of faith in this particular version of the Christian Church. But for many of us (unrepentant) Protestant liberals, the second is asking too much. The historic creeds all affirm faith in the Church, and one can join in this affirmation without giving a precise juridical definition of where this Church is located in the murky flow of human events.

If Christianity is true, then the universe is in the final analysis a vast liturgy in praise of its creator. It was created for this purpose and it *is* this purpose. This liturgy includes all human beings who have been brought to this understanding and (in the "inclusivist" version of religious plurality) it also includes those who praise God under strange names. The cosmic liturgy includes the living and the dead, and it includes the angels and all beings in this or any other world. If Christianity is true, then the one who affirms this truth must necessarily join the community of praise. This community must also have embodiments in the world of human beings—that is, there must be places where people gather to worship, by whatever means available. In other words, the cosmic community of praise must necessarily have empirical manifestations. What divides theological liberals not only from Catholics but from just about any other version of orthodoxy is the degree of specificity one wants to impose on these empirical manifestations.

Paul Tillich coined the phrase "the Protestant principle" to denote the Reformers' insistence that the empirical Church must not be absolutized, that it is always in need of reform (*ecclesia semper reformanda*). In comparison with the juridical ecclesiology of Rome this Protestant principle constitutes a considerable relativization of the historically shaped Church. In Lutheran language, the boundaries of the Church could not be drawn in an abstract juridical manner; rather it was to be found "wherever the Gospel is correctly preached and the sacraments are correctly administered." Needless to say, the adverb "correctly" in this formula opened up another, in the end no less juridical way of specifying the empirical boundaries of the Church in the history of Lutheran orthodoxy. I think one can say that Protestant liberalism carried the relativization a step further. It suggests a much looser, less specific understanding of how the community of worship of the galaxies and all the archangels may find a habitation in the world of men. One could still, I suppose, use the old Lutheran language, giving a much more liberal interpretation to the slippery adverb. But perhaps another Lutheran formula might be useful here, one that originally referred to the sacraments.

In differentiating themselves both from the Swiss Reformers and from Rome, the early Lutherans proposed that Christ was present in the eucharist "in, with, and under" the empirical elements of bread and wine. The Roman understanding, sharpened even further in the debates with Protestantism, was quite different. It proposed a miraculous transformation of the empirical elements, caught very well in the term "transsubstantiation." The Swiss, by contrast, proposed that the eucharist was merely symbolic, a commemoration of what originally occurred when Jesus last supped with his disciples. I would suggest that the formula has much broader applicability. It is useful in reflecting on God's presence in the empirical world and in the community that proclaims Him through Christ.

One can understand the Church as a miracle. In doing so, of course, one does not have to overlook the often sordid empirical manifestations of what, underneath it all, is a miraculous reality. On the contrary, one might even say that the more sordid the empirical manifestations, the more wonderful the miracle. Thus the unsavory realities of the Borgia Vatican, or Torquemada and the Inquisition, and of a long line of drunken bishops, imbecile theologians, and even criminal popes need not undermine the believing Catholic's faith that, despite all this, God intended this particular community to hold the keys to salvation until Christ returns in glory. To use the word in an originally unintended way, such faith "transsubstantiates" the world. It posits the primacy of the invisible even in the here and now of an as yet only partially redeemed world. The visible world (of bread and wine, of popes and cardinals) appears unchanged, but that is only appearance: Behind the visible facade a great miracle has occurred and, precisely through the Church, is occurring again and again. This miracle was begun by Jesus, and handed on through the apostles to a long succession of bishops (among whom the pope has primacy) down to this day.

By contrast, one can in the "Swiss" manner understand the Church as a purely empirical phenomenon, as a gathering of human beings who wish to commemorate a particular tradition, to encourage and perhaps inspire each other. Such an understanding need not be secularized (it certainly was not even in the case of the more radical Swiss Protestants), though it often is today. The tradition being commemorated may be anything but secular; there may be prayers and sermons full of supernatural references. But the empirical community has no status other than the obvious sociological one. Paradoxically, such an understanding of the Church leads to *less* tolerance of human foibles in comparison with the Catholic view, rather than more as one would first expect. Upon reflection the paradox resolves itself. If one believes in the Church as a miracle, one can put up with any number of warts on those who are supposed to be in charge of it. If, on the other hand, the Church is understood as a gathering of high-minded people without the benefit of any miraculous interventions, then they had better be high-minded or the whole enterprise will cease to be plausible.

If one applies the Lutheran formula to the question of the Church (admittedly in a liberal vein that would have shocked its inventors), then one arrives at a position somewhere in the middle between the miraculous and the sociological views. The former asks us to believe too much, the latter too little. It is too much, I think, to accept all the warts of the Roman centuries in the name of an authority whose historical claims are dubious and whose present reality is very ambiguous. But on the other hand, it is a belittling understanding of Christianity that omits its relation to the cosmos, that sees the redemption it proclaims as merely human, and its visible community as only a sociological phenomenon. It is possible to believe that Christ is present in the Church "in, with, and under" its often depressing empirical elements. The bread is stale and the wine is sour. There is no miracle, no transsubstantiation. But there is also far more than a commemorative celebration. There is the real connection with the angels, with the cosmic choir that stretches through all the stars and beyond into realities utterly beyond our comprehension. And, needless to add, the earthly adumbrations of this eternal liturgy may take different forms, speak different languages, and sometimes bear little resemblance to the great historic traditions of the Christian faith.

From this perspective, the answer to the question as to *which* church one should join remains indefinite.

There is no authoritative answer that applies to everyone. Again using traditional Protestant language, one might say that ecclesial belonging is a matter of "vocation," of what one may singularly be called upon to do. Vocations differ. It may be a legitimate Christian vocation to continue in one's original community, even if that community has become a very unappealing place. It may be equally legitimate to change one's ecclesial affiliation in a direction that promises less frustration. One may be called to inner emigration and one may also be called (as Simone Weil eloquently argued for herself) to the role of a solitary outsider. Vocations are relative by definition. This relativization does indeed have a peculiar, perhaps disturbing affinity with the sociological realities of modern pluralism. What I am suggesting here is that we shouldn't be overly disturbed. It is a traditional, indeed orthodox Christian insight that God often works in strange ways. If in days of old He could work through the Assyrians and equally unappealing agents, it is not unthinkable that He can work today through the social and cognitive structures of the pluralizing consumer culture.

8

The Problem of Moral Action

Pluralism undermines all certainties. In terms of everyday living, the effects of this are probably most disturbing in the matter of morality, because moral considerations enter into most human actions most of the time. A good many people manage to put aside the "deeper" questions as they go about the business of living and in doing so they insulate themselves against the crisis that pluralism has inflicted on religion. Such insulation is more difficult when it comes to morality. American society as a whole has succeeded reasonably well in coping with religious pluralism, despite the tensions and discontents discussed earlier. However, American society is having a difficult time coping with the moral pluralism that has now quite loudly come to the fore. The abortion issue sharply illustrates this difficulty. It is correctly seen as a profoundly moral issue by all parties. Survey data on the issue are unreliable; more than usually, a lot depends on how the question is put to the people surveyed. Yet it is clear that a substantial segment of the American population regards abortion as an act of homicide while another substantial segment sees it as a fundamental human right of women. Not surprisingly, there is intense fervor on both sides and compromise, that great pluralist virtue, is not readily imaginable. This issue also illustrates the linkage between the religious and the moral dimensions of pluralism, as clergy and religious activists are prominently engaged on both sides of the dispute. Nevertheless, there is a widespread expectation that religion will somehow provide the firm moral guidance that will rescue us from the relativizations of pluralism. Religion is still looked to by many people as the one likely source for morally reliable guideposts amid the confusions of a pluralistic age.

Behind this expectation lies a conventional view of the relation between religion and morality, which holds that the latter depends on the former. Morality is supposed to derive from religion. In a stronger version of this view, *only* religion can provide a reliable basis for morality. There is further a conventional Christian specification to the effect that only Christianity can provide a reliable body of moral principles to live by. The details of these principles, of course, differ greatly between different denominations, ranging from notions of natural law, through the fundamentalist belief that the Bible supplies a clear moral law, to the liberal idea that Christian ethics is always "contextual." Curiously, though, all these positions share the underlying assumption about the inextricable linkage between religion and morality.

Once again, there is a paradox. Yes, religion and morality are linked. If one looks at moral systems throughout human history, most of them (in fact, nearly all) were legitimated in religious terms. Human beings were instructed to do this and to refrain from that *because* these instructions derive from the gods or, more abstractly, from a divinely founded order of the universe. But no, religion and morality are not necessarily linked. If one analyzes the character of religious experience (I would again refer to Rudolf Otto), its innermost core has nothing to do with morality at all. All morality is directed toward the reality of everyday life; religious experience transcends that reality radically, is directed toward an *other* reality in which, by definition, moral principles and rules are irrelevant.

The paradox can be resolved, I think, by focusing on the relation between what I have called normative and cognitive definitions of reality. The former tell us how to act, the latter what the world is like. I think one can show that all normative definitions depend upon specific cognitive definitions. For example: The incest tabu is probably the most ancient moral principle. Most generally defined, it is a norm that tells me I may not marry a close relative. But who is a close relative? In a particular society the norm may be specified by telling me that I may not marry a fifth cousin. In order to follow this norm, or even to make sense of it, I must know just *who are* my fifth cousins. In other words, the normative definition "incest is wrong" depends on a set of cognitive definitions of the nature of kinship, which in turn probably rest on further cognitive definitions about the nature of human beings, about social order and perhaps about the basic structure of the universe. Another example: Pro-life advocates tell us that every life is sacred; pro-choice advocates tell us of the sacred right of every women to control her body. Yet both normative declarations presuppose cognitive assumptions without which they make no sense. The pro-life assumption is that a six-day old fetus is a person entitled to the full protection of the law; the pro-choice assumption is that a six-*month* old fetus is simply a part of a woman's body. Both positions are based on specific assumptions that are cognitive rather than normative or moral, assumptions about what *is* rather than what *ought to be*. As this example shows, any debate over morality will be fruitless unless there is some agreement about the realities to which the morality refers.

Religion defines the nature of reality. In that sense, religion is *cognitive*: It tells us what *is*. Furthermore, religion defines reality in the most ample way possible. Its definition embraces all that is, including of course the realities of everyday life. This is the meaning of the old phrase that the Christian views everything *sub specie aeternitatis*, "in the perspective of eternity." Once the world is seen in the light of what Christian faith discloses about it, relations between human beings must also be placed in that all-embracing frame of reference. Inevitably, there must be moral implications to this. Thus, to mention only the most basic, if I believe (amazingly enough) that God cares for me, it follows that He also cares for all my fellow men; this will inevitably have moral implications for how I ought to deal with them. Needless to say, this sort of effect is not limited to Christianity. If, say, I believe in the Hindu view of reality as dominated by *samsara*, the endless cycle of incarnations, then this view will inevitably affect my understanding of *dharma*, the moral obligations I have in

society. And so on. Seen this way, there is indeed a linkage between religion and morality. But it is a rather far
cry from the linkage assumed by those who believe that
a particular legal code or moral canon was directly given
by the gods, or for that matter by a natural law inscribed
in all human beings.

It is a truism to point out that the most divergent
and often diametrically opposed moral imperatives
have been legitimated in Christian terms. I will mention
only the most dramatic case of this in my own experience. It was in the late 1950s and I was on my very first
teaching job at an institution in the South. Two events
occurred in the town where I was teaching within the
span of a few weeks—a visit by Martin Luther King, Jr.,
who was then beginning his great civil rights movement, and (possibly not unconnected) a rally of the Ku
Klux Klan. The first event took place in a black church
and I was much impressed by the religious quality of
the proceedings. Both before and after King's speech
there were prayers, Bible readings, and hymns. The
hymns were mostly old Protestant revival hymns, including "Rock of Ages" and "The Old Rugged Cross."
The KKK rally was on the outskirts of town, and I went
with a faculty colleague, with some trepidation. In the
event nothing very terrifying occurred, other than the
thoroughly repulsive rhetoric. Indeed, the proceedings,
like those at the black church, were marked by a specifically Protestant type of collective jolliness (John Murray Cuddihy has aptly named this "the Protestant
smile"). The climax of the rally, of course, consisted of
the lighting of the cross. My hair stood on end when,
of all hymns, this congregation began to sing "The Old
Rugged Cross."

I want to make the point carefully, so as not to be
misunderstood. The story by no means implies a moral
equivalence between the two causes. Then as now I

would accept the Christian basis of the civil rights movement and deny any such basis to the ideology of hatred represented by the KKK. But that is beside the point here. Rather it is that the *very same* symbols of an old-fashioned Southern Protestantism were used to legitimate two diametrically opposed political causes. The case is hardly unique in Christian history. Virtually every time that so-called Christian nations have gone to war with each other, ecclesial officials blessed the banners of the opposing armies with identical Christian symbols. The same is true of other religious traditions. Again, the point is not that all causes that men have fought over are therefore morally equivalent. Emphatically, they are not. The point is that, to put it mildly, religious legitimations, including those proposed in Christian terms, are extraordinarily flexible. They can easily be bent this way or that, to consecrate just about any cause. Most of these legitimations are what German philosophers have called *Leerformeln*—"empty formulas" so abstract that they can be filled with any momentarily convenient content. The exceptions are cases where the religiously grounded injunctions are very specific; "You may not marry your fifth cousin." Where such specificity occurs, many Christians will reject it as some kind of fundamentalism—and other Christians, especially sophisticated ones, will find a way of distinguishing *some* fifth cousins who may be married after all.

One of the strategies employed by liberal Protestants and others to avoid dealing with the cognitively embarrassing supernatural elements in the Christian tradition has been to focus on its alleged ethical core. In other words, the strategy has been to translate theology into ethics. I have earlier expressed the view that, as a strategy, this is self-defeating. My point here, however, is that analysis of the tradition fails to yield such an ethical core, except in very general terms. A favorite exercise of liberal theologians in the late nineteenth- and early twentieth-centuries, until New Testament scholarship made this more and more difficult, was to explicate the so-called "ethic of Jesus" as the core of Christianity. New Testament scholars are no more given to consensus than any other group of intellectuals, but it is safe to say that two results of their work have made it increasingly difficult to focus on the "ethic of Jesus." One has been the discovery that Jesus' moral teachings were far less original than had previously been thought. To be sure, Jesus had some original ways of putting things and he had a way of radicalizing moral points, but the greater part of his ethical teachings can be derived from various Jewish sources. The other and probably more important result of New Testament scholarship has been the insight that Jesus was very little concerned with ethics in the first place. His message was not about morality. Rather, as he reiterated over and over again, it was to announce the onset of the Kingdom of God, a cataclysmic event that would radically change the whole world. Insofar as this implies an "ethic," it is a set of guidelines for people to prepare for the cataclysm and wait for it in a proper manner. Ferdinand Mount, in his book *The Subversive Family*, argues that Christianity, with its totalistic demands, has always been anti-family. In one of his nastier asides, after conceding that the Sermon on the Mount is indeed admirable, he observes that it must have been written for bachelors, since no one with family obligations could possibly live by it. One may doubt Mount's thesis about the anti-family bias in Christianity, but the point about bachelors is well taken. One could amplify it: The Sermon on the Mount is a set of instructions to bachelors on how to spend the last week before the end of the world. This does not detract from its sublimity, but it seriously detracts from the possibility of making the "ethic of Jesus" the focus of Christian faith today.

I am inclined to think that the relationship of Christian faith and morality is more indirect, and that it once again can be best understood in terms of the dependence of normative on cognitive definitions of reality. What happened in the early Christian community was a radical shift in the perception of reality. If one is to give credence to at least some accounts in the Gospels and the Book of Acts (and I think that one must), then this shift occurred abruptly, suddenly, following right in the wake of the utter defeat and despair of Jesus' death. The events of Easter and Pentecost, impossible though they are to reconstruct with the methods of historical scholarship, must either have caused or ratified this shift. Thus the earliest Christian confessions of faith—that God was in Christ and that this Christ had risen from the dead—dramatically transformed the view of the world. God, who had created the world, had entered it, suffered, and died in it, and had once and for all triumphed over suffering, sin, and death; furthermore, the benefits of this mighty drama of redemption were now available to every human being who has faith. This is a cognitive revolution, not a normative one. There is no new law here, no new code of morality or ethical philosophy. But normative implications follow inevitably from this cognitive shift. Some came to view right away; others took time, even centuries, to become fully conscious. And the basic normative implication, though it applies to hundreds of different human situations, is of awesome simplicity—that every human being has immeasurable worth, as God has shown us by His immeasurable act of redemption.

Frederick Neumann once made a curious observation: We usually think of conscience as speaking in the imperative—"do this," "don't do that." But this is a distortion; conscience speaks in the indicative—*it points*. I think there is an important insight in this, even if the observation may not exhaust the deeply puzzling phenomenon of conscience. Our sense that we ought to act in a certain way and to refrain from other actions is triggered, so to speak, by *scenes that come into view* and that carry with them these moral implications. Someone once said that the mother of a newborn infant is in a morally privileged position, because she knows exactly what God wants her to do. But this is not because God has instructed her as to her proper behavior in the situation, by whatever set of imperative norms, but because *the infant is there* and being there it calls for protection, care, and love. Conversely, there are scenes that present themselves as calling for moral condemnation and redress, as in Dostoyevsky's famous example of the absolute necessity of stopping an act of cruelty to a child. The example can be multiplied indefinitely in terms of the many scenes of human cruelty, oppression, and injustice. Conscience points us to these scenes, and by pointing bids us both to condemn and to act in redress or resistance. Now, what we do know very well (and modern historical, social-scientific, and psychological studies have amply demonstrated) is that not all consciences are the same, or more specifically that conscience is shaped by the forces of history, culture, and individual biography. In other words, just what conscience points us toward is relative in terms of one's location. I doubt that any theory of natural law can adequately cope with this pervasive fact of moral relativity. In the course of history, though, it is clear that the different religious traditions have been crucial in shaping specific forms of conscience. Put simply, different worldviews point to different occasions calling for moral judgment. The Christian view of the world, over and over through the centuries, has pointed the conscience of individuals to scenes where the immeasurable worth of human beings has been denied or trampled upon. Christian conscience, I think, mainly expresses itself in a voice that says "no!" or more precisely that says "look on this scene—it should not be!"

This is a long way from any legalistic interpretation of Christian ethics. Curiously, though, it is just this kind of indicative insight that can lead to a sense of absolute conviction, or as close to absoluteness as any of us can attain. Thus, to return to Dostoyevsky's example, the conviction that it is wrong to torture a child is absolute. It requires no intellectual proof, not even an act of faith. It demands any action necessary to stop the torturer and it will inflict incontrovertible guilt if such action is not taken. Again, we know very well that this is not so with all human beings, not in the past and, alas, not today either. But the unfolding of the Christian view of the world, of God and of man, inexorably led to this conviction. Christianity shaped conscience, which then insisted on pointing at scenes that, once looked at, became morally intolerable. Once this insight is gained, it becomes itself part of a view of the world. As has become evident, that view can be detached from the religious faith that first engendered it. All sorts of people who have no allegiance to Christianity now share this view. This does not make them "anonymous Christians" (in Karl Rahner's sense). But the fact can be interpreted in a simple but far-reaching manner: Christian faith has been instrumental in discovering certain truths about the human condition, and truth authenticates itself.

These considerations lead to a somewhat surprising if tentative conclusion: While the pluralistic situation plunges both religion and morality into a crisis of
relativization, for most of us the possibility of achieving
some moral certainties is greater than that of achieving
religious certainty. The reason for this should be evident. Once conscience points us toward certain scenes,
these are directly, empirically available to us in a way
that transcendence is not. The torturer and his victim
are fellow beings in the world of social reality. They may
be physically present or we may know about them
through various information media. In either case, at
least potentially, they are possible objects of our own
actions—directly if they are physically present, indi-
rectly if they are not. This empirical availability makes
possible a certitude that is much harder to come by in
the area of religion. Perhaps, in terms of strict logic, the
affirmations of moral perception ("it is absolutely wrong
to torture a child") may also require an act of faith, comparable to religious faith ("I believe that God was in
Christ"). But if we put the phrase "I believe" in front of
the affirmation about the wrongness of torture, we are,
I think, distorting the nature of this moral perception: I
don't really *believe* that this act is evil—I *know* it. Therefore, unlike my readiness to respectfully consider just
about any religious proposition, I would refuse to engage in polite dialogue with torturers or with those who
defend torture. It seems to me that, almost instinctively,
most people in our pluralistic situation are aware of this
difference. The public will perhaps be amused but not
shocked by a talk-show host saying, "So, Mr. Smith,
you believe that cabbages and only cabbages are rein-
carnated human beings. This is very interesting. Can
you tell us more about it?" I do not think that many
persons will sit still for a similar dialogue with Mr.

Smith whose hobby is torturing children. The conscience of the West has been shaped by such insights. The horrors of totalitarianism, itself a product of Western civilization, may be cited as a counter-argument. But it is not persuasive. Thus the Nazis (the counter-argument *par excellence*) not only had to engage in a massive and continuous propaganda effort, supported by pervasive fear, to make their barbaric morality seem acceptable; despite all of this, they were careful to perpetrate their horrors in great secrecy, shielded as much as possible from public view.

When Simone Weil was looking for a refuge in Nazi-occupied France, she found it on the farm of Gustave Thibon, apparently a rather cranky Catholic intellectual devoted to a rustic life. In an introduction to a posthumously published collection of essays by Weil, Thibon confesses that, although he was never an anti-Semite, he had never gotten along well with Jews, that he disliked people who were politically on the left, and that he was particularly suspicious of professional philosophers. He subsequently came to respect the awkward young woman who arrived at his house with the completely unrealistic offer to work there as a farmhand, but that was not the reason he agreed to take her in before he had ever met her. He did so because he considered it a self-evident duty toward an individual who was being unjustly persecuted, despite the fact that such an act would subject him to considerable risk. There were a good many such cases in Europe during the dark days of Nazi rule. But, alas, they were the rare exceptions in a generally dismal story of prudent avoidance of involvement if not indifference or even collaboration. The exceptional cases are inspiring precisely because they are evidence of moral certainty in the face of self-evident evil. We feel encouraged by them in an age of deepening moral relativism. It is probably correct to say that the development of this relativism has progressed considerably in the half-century since World War II.

It would be misleading to downplay this development, which is precisely the effect of pluralism in the moral sphere. It is a very serious problem. All the same, it seems to me that here, too, pluralism is a challenge and not just an affliction. The relativization of moral convictions in many areas of life forces reflection, just as religious pluralism does. Reflection can be painful; it can also be liberating. The pluralistic situation makes possible a *prise de conscience* in the moral sphere; it should be noted that in French the word "conscience" has both a normative and a cognitive referent. The phrase might be freely translated as *a recollection of what we know.*

If we turn again to the contemporary Christian scene, two modern versions of Christian morality predominate. These may be called the legalistic and the utopian. Both, I believe, are misunderstandings, at least if one takes one's cue from the New Testament. The Pauline Epistles provide us with a very different understanding—non-legalistic without being relativistic and non-utopian without lacking concern for the welfare of human beings. It is an understanding based on the "new being in Christ"—that is, on an existence that results from the shift in the perception of reality brought about by Christian faith. It is a precarious, vulnerable existence, precisely because it is based on faith. Both legalism and utopianism are attempts to shore up the precariousness by some sort of security. In a Pauline understanding of Christian existence, this is a false security and it finally expresses lack of faith.

Most forms of Christian orthodoxy today tend toward legalism. Roman Catholics believe in the *magisterium* of the Church extending authoritatively to every area of moral choice. Evangelical Protestants substitute the Bible for the Church as an infallible moral guide. If one can bring oneself to credit either proposition, things fall into place with a degree of neatness: Once again, or so it seems, one knows exactly what one ought to do. Thus, to take an important example, there appears to be a greatly reassuring certainty as to what one should and should not do regarding sexual behavior. The relativizing processes of our age have brought a high degree of confusion into this area, extending from overt behavior into what has come to be called "gender identity"—just what it means to be a man or a woman, or for that matter how to make sense of a "sexual orientation" that does not fit comfortably under either category. If one can bring oneself to believe in these authorities, it is a great "unburdening" (one might even say, ironically, a "liberation") to be able to organize one's behavior in accordance with what the Church teaches or with what the Bible supposedly says, down to the details.

It is a very widespread view among theologically liberal people that religious institutions that try to regulate their members' lives will lose credibility. In other words, the "difficult" churches will lose out. There is an element of validity to this notion. Thus there is strong evidence for the view that the Roman Catholic church has lost credibility and indeed lost members because of its "difficult" teachings in the area of sexual behavior, especially concerning contraception. On the whole, however, the opposite view seems more plausible. This is particularly evident as one looks at Protestantism; here the "difficult" churches are showing growth and robust vitality, while the "easy" ones are losing both vitality and members. Probably the root explanation of this puzzle lies at the heart of religious psychology: A god who asks nothing of me is unlikely to do much for me. Put differently: The plausibility of any definition of reality increases in the measure that allegiance requires sacrifice (which, for instance, is why Freud insisted that his patients pay fees).

Utopianism at first blush seems to be a different phenomenon altogether. Here the alleged Christian ethic becomes commitment to a program of mundane improvement and a legalistic ordering of personal behavior need not be included in the program. In principle, the program could have any content whatsoever, be it explicitly political or more generally concerned to bring about social change. Thus what Christianity supposedly demands of us morally may be to bring about revolution, or suppress revolution; to free one's nation from foreign domination, or impose domination on another nation. It could also be to change the relations between the sexes, save the natural environment, eradicate economic and racial injustice, or cleanse society of alcohol, tobacco, or cholesterol. Whatever the utopian campaign, it wonderfully simplifies the moral economy. While one is working for the revolution or making war on one's demons there may still be unrelated moral norms that command attention, such as not sleeping with the wrong people. But these matters unrelated to the utopian project are, by definition, less important, almost trivial. Finally, what is moral is determined by whatever serves the cause; all actions are finally judged in terms of their serviceability. But this too constitutes a great moral "unburdening" which makes it much easier to enact moral choices. Thus both legalism and utopianism supply magnificent *simplifications* for the moral life, and this accounts for their enduring attraction.

In principle, utopian programs can be of the left or of the right, or indeed of no politically locatable character. For sociological reasons that cannot be entered into here, the utopian ideas that have proved most attractive in recent Christian history have either been of the left or have felt most at home in a generally left ambience. Thus liberation theology, in its original Latin American version, was a deliberate attempt to incorporate a Marxist understanding of the contemporary world within a Christian program of moral action. Marxism has not had a very happy time in the last few years, but the ideas on social ethics dominant among mainline Protestant as well as Roman Catholic intellectuals and Church bureaucrats continue to be broadly left-of-center. The same *gauchiste* sentiments also mark utopian movements that, in strict logic, would not have to be on the left politically, such as the radical wings of feminists, gay liberationists, environmentalists, and black nationalists in this country. Another point that should be stressed is that, of course, not all utopian programs today are religiously affiliated or legitimated. On the contrary, most modern utopianism has been of a secular character (in the case of left utopians, often militantly so) and the Christians who have embraced utopian causes have usually not invented these. Thus the worldview espoused by liberation theologians was taken over *in toto* from the highly secular, indeed atheist tradition of Marxism; what the theologians did was to announce a moral duty to enlist in the political activity called for by this Marxist analysis.

It seems to me that Christian faith suggests a moral stance that is *neither* legalistic *nor* utopian. This stance was best understood by Paul in the early days of the Christian era and it was powerfully regained in the Protestant Reformation in the sixteenth century, especially in its Lutheran version. I cannot fully expand on this position here, but suffice it to say that, in my understanding, both legalism and utopianism greatly diminish the reality-transforming power of the Christian experience. The former does so by reducing Christianity to yet another moral system, the latter by reducing it to a mundane campaign differentiated from others less by its content than by the uncompromising ferocity of those committed to it. Each in its own way, both legalism and utopianism curiously *secularize* the Christian Gospel, shifting its message from transcendence to the affairs of this world. I believe this is a grandiose misunderstanding of the New Testament itself as well as of a core tradition of Christian experience and thought over the centuries. But the Kingdom of God, which Jesus announced in his earthly ministry and which his disciples experienced in the events that followed Easter, is *not* of this world.

Max Weber, in his famous essay, "Politics as a Vocation," distinguishes between an "ethic of sentiment" (*Gesinnungsethik*) and an "ethic of responsibility" (*Verantwortungsethik*). Both provide criteria for the moral assessment of actions, but the criteria are very different. An "ethic of sentiment" judges the moral status of an action by the intention motivating the actor. An "ethic of responsibility" does so by looking at the probable consequences of the action. As an exemplar of the former type Weber cites Tolstoy, an absolute pacifist who would forgo the use of violence no matter what the consequences. This has been a common pacifist position ever since, though of course the same ethical position can be taken with regard to actions that do not involve the possible use of violence. As an exemplar of the latter type of ethic Weber quotes Machiavelli, who praised the statesman who would sacrifice his salvation for the welfare of his city. That is an overly strong statement. It can be put more moderately by saying that an individual acting by such an ethic puts the welfare of others above his own moral purity. In the sphere of political action especially, this means accepting the fact that there are situations where it is morally unavoidable to get one's hands dirty, even bloody. This insight is not uncommon among people who are actively involved in the affairs of the world. The popularity of John le Carré's novels may perhaps be explained by his reiteration of the same insight. His melancholy secret agents, caught in the dreary violence of espionage and covert operations, constantly reflect about the impossibility of keeping clean hands in this world.

A strictly legalistic ethic avoids the Weberian dichotomy: If one only follows the dictates of the "law" (whatever that may be), neither one's sentiments nor the consequences of one's actions need enter the moral calculus as principal criteria. In the absence of a legalistic ethic, Weber's dichotomy holds. It holds for the Christian who rejects the notion that the teachings of Jesus or of the Bible as a whole or of the Church provide such a "law," a reliable and generally applicable code of conduct. Which of Weber's two ethical possibilities is then more plausible? I would contend that it must be, unambiguously, the second. On the Day of Judgment, we may presume, our sentiments, motives, and intentions will be taken into account. In the meantime, in this world they are of little if any moral interest. Christian faith mandates an overriding concern for our neighbors, *not* for the purity of our selves. More than that, the latter concern is a morally deplorable self-indulgence, especially when coupled with a lack of thought for the consequences of our supposedly pure actions.

In recent years the aforementioned dichotomy has been much in evidence in the debate over the place of human rights in American foreign policy. This debate has also taken place in other democracies, but it is particularly sharp in the United States because of a distinctive utopian tradition going back to the twin sources of the American political ethos, Puritanism and the Enlightenment. The case of torture was mentioned before; it may serve here too. There are, alas, a good number of countries in the world whose governments routinely use torture as a means of political coercion. One position maintains that the proper response to such governments is public condemnation, coupled with pressures ranging from economic boycott to military intervention. Another position holds that none of these means should be ruled out in principle, if American power and interests so dictate, but that the real chances of success for such actions must always be the foremost consideration, especially the chances of actually changing the behavior of these governments and thus helping their victims. In that case the chosen course may well be to refrain from public condemnation, and to rely on quiet diplomacy or other means that are not immediately visible. Most important, the latter position will always insist on a calculus of probable consequences, even while understanding that very often it is difficult to assess the probability. In a number of cases (Iran and Nicaragua have been prominent) a human rights policy based on sentiment rather than on a calculus of consequences has led to the overthrow of an odious regime, which was promptly succeeded by a regime greatly more odious.

One can adopt an "ethic of responsibility" even if one is convinced of the absolute evil that torture represents. There may well be a Christian vocation to be nothing but a witness against such evils, with no thought of practicalities or consequences. In other words, there may be an authentically Christian option to be like Tolstoy. In Christian history this option, more properly called a vocation, was the monastic one, and I for one think that an unfortunate result of the Reformation was its disappearance in Protestantism. But most of us are not called to a monastic life. And especially if we are called to political action (which, in principle is the calling of every citizen in a democracy), the Tolstoyan option is not viable, indeed may do very great harm. The Kingdom of God is not of this world; conversely, this world is not yet the Kingdom of God. It is a very dirty world. Yet it is in this world that our actions must play themselves out. There is no way that we can avoid dirty hands.

The classical Protestant understanding of these issues was resolutely non-utopian. I think the Lutheran understanding was the clearest within the Protestant universe of discourse, and also the most directly grounded in Paul's view of the Christian condition. Lutheran theology expressed this understanding in the doctrine of the two kingdoms, which in turn was rooted in the doctrine of justification by faith alone. The kingdom of grace is yet to come, though it is foreshadowed in the community gathered around the proclamation of the Gospel. In this world we can at best seek the kingdom of justice—and justice in this world is always imperfect, relative, tainted by human sin and folly. Nor are we justified by works, by our actions in the world. Justified by faith alone, we yet remain sinners. Thus the Christian is always and at the same time both just and sinning, *simul iustus et peccator*. There is a great liberation in this understanding of moral action. It frees us both from legalistic anxiety and from the self-centered concern for our own moral purity. It frees us to do the best we can in a very imperfect world and to rely on God's forgiveness when, almost inevitably, we fail to achieve our most well-meaning projects. And the criterion of what is best, quite simply, will be the best chance to decrease the amount of injustice in the world; in other words, the criterion will always be what our actions do for others, not ourselves.

Nothing that has been said here makes the crisis brought on by moral pluralism disappear. Just as religious certainty is hard to come by in the pluralistic age, so is moral certainty. What I may perceive as a clear and unambiguous injustice may not be so perceived by others with whom I interact every day, and this fact inevitably puts what may be called cognitive pressure on my own perception. In the earlier discussion of religious experience I emphasized the element of trust—trust, that is, in my own experience. The same observation applies to my moral experience—those clear perceptions, usually negative, to which my conscience points. The perception of torture as an unmitigated evil may serve as a paradigmatic moral experience. I trust in this experience. Since I am a social being, my trust will very probably waver if I find myself in the company of people who believe otherwise. What I must do then is undertake the previously mentioned *prise de conscience*—to recollect what I know, and have faith that what I know is truth. This is not a formula for immunity against the corrosive effects of relativity. If relativity is a stormy sea of uncertainties, this faith does not magically make the waters recede so that we can march through them on a dry path. What it does do is give us the courage to set sail on our little boat, with the hope that, by God's grace, we will reach the other shore without drowning.

Epilogue:
The Burden of Silence

A t the conclusion of his famous essay on "Science as a Vocation," Max Weber makes some rather patronizing remarks about those who return penitently into the arms of the traditional churches, and he affirms his own determination to face up without evasions to the disenchantment of the world. The great German sociologist once called himself "religiously unmusical." This sounds somewhat disingenuous, coming as it does from a man who spent the bulk of his scholarly work on the careful and highly empathetic study of many religious expressions. Be this as it may, here he rejects the, as he thought, easy consolations of religion in favor of a relentless intellectual honesty and a willingness to meet the challenge of an age without prophets. Yet, in a somewhat opaque way, he admits to a certain longing for such authoritative proclaimers of truth. And then, curiously, he quotes a passage from the twenty-first chapter of the Book of Isaiah, a passage he describes (probably accurately) as an old watchman's song that somehow found its way into this book of the Hebrew Bible. It is a very short but strangely evocative passage:

> The oracle concerning Dumah.
> One is calling to me from Se'ir,
> "Watchman, what of the night?
>   Watchman, what of the night?"
> The watchman says:
> "Morning comes, and also the night.
>   If you will inquire, inquire;
>   come back again."

This is an obscure text, and one must wonder why Weber fastened on it in the context of one of his most important statements on the role of the scientist in the modern world. The text is found in the midst of a collection of oracles directed against different peoples of the ancient Near East. The Revised Standard Version, whose text I quoted, quite correctly heads the passage with the word "oracle." The literal translation from the Hebrew, which is how the Authorized Version translates the heading, would read "The burden of Dumah." While it is quite true that, in the prophetic form of language employed here, "burden" means the weight of an oracle directed against this or that object of God's wrath, I think that here is a case where the older literal rendering is much to be preferred. "The burden of Dumah": What is it? Who bore it? Is it our burden too?

The biblical Book of Isaiah is more of a library than a single book. While it is dominated by two gigantic figures, the First Isaiah and the much more recent Deutero-Isaiah, various other texts have been incorporated into the book that bears the most august name in Israelite prophecy (such sheltering under a great name, of course, was a very common practice among ancient scribes). However obscure the present text, one thing about it is clear, namely that it could come from neither of the two mighty Isaiahs. It is written in a mixture of Hebrew and Aramaic, which points to a recent date in terms of the Hebrew Bible, possibly the fifth or fourth century before the Christian era (Weber thought it came from the period of the Babylonian exile, which is almost certainly too old). Se'ir is a stretch of hill country southeast of the Dead Sea belonging to the Edomites, and it is also used synonymously with Edom. It is possible, given this location, that the song or poem in the text is of Edomite origin (again, Weber thought so). It seems plausible that the text does indeed come from a watchman's song. On the face of it, it contains an exchange between a night watchman and the narrator, who is anxious for the coming of the morning.

We know where Se'ir and Edom were. Both, separately or synonymously, are mentioned a number of times in the Hebrew Bible. According to the Book of Joshua this land was given by God to Esau, the brother of the patriarch Jacob (perhaps, one might surmise, as compensation for the patrimony that Jacob cheated his brother out of). But we don't know where Dumah was, or even whether it was a place at all. I make no pretense whatever to biblical scholarship, but I'll take the risk of voicing a preference. The literal meaning of Dumah is "silence." If for a moment we hypothesize that this is *not* a place, the heading of the passage could now be literally rendered as "the burden of silence." If we do this, the passage is suddenly filled with meaning. And we can also see why Weber was fascinated by it.

This meaning suggests itself if we look at one rather prominent biblical passage in which Se'ir is mentioned; since the passage is from the Pentateuch, it would certainly have been known to whoever thought of inserting this little ditty into the Book of Isaiah. The passage is part of the blessing given by Moses just before his death, as reported in the thirty-third chapter of Deuteronomy:

The Lord came from Sinai,
and dawned from Se'ir upon us;
he shone forth from Mount Paran,
he came from the ten thousands of holy ones,
with flaming fire at his right hand.

Moses here reminds Israel of the great deeds of the God who brought it out of Egypt, gave it the law at Sinai, fed it in the wilderness, and led it to the promised land. This passage, which is the beginning of a long chapter in which each tribe receives a special blessing, speaks of one or more hierophanies, or powerful manifestations, of Yahweh. After Sinai, the climax of the revelation mediated by Moses to Israel, Yahweh is said to have dawned over the hills of Se'ir. What a total contrast with the mention of Se'ir in Isaiah! In Deuteronomy, Se'ir appears in the context of an overwhelming presence of God, "with flaming fire at his right hand." In Isaiah, the one who calls from Se'ir speaks of no flaming fire, no thousands of holy beings, indeed does not mention God at all. Instead, there is just the weary question asked of the watchman about the coming of morning. One is almost tempted to say that Se'ir has becomes secularized between these two texts, from a locale of God's revelation to a place where people sit and wait in darkness. The glory of God's manifestations now seems very far away.

"The burden of silence": Is it too fanciful to suggest that this is the silence that has fallen on Se'ir after God has departed? It is the silence when God no longer speaks. *That* is the burden. And what a terrible burden it has been at so many moments in the history of Israel!

It is sobering to reflect that whatever probable date we would finally assign to this text, say from the sixth to the fourth centuries, there would be only few and relatively short periods during which we could not easily imagine Jewish individuals desperately wishing that God would break His silence. And so it would be in all the centuries of Jewish history since then, down to the horrors of our own century. "What of the night?" the watchman is asked. Presumably this is a way of asking what time it is. The question is not asked, we may presume, out of an impersonal need to know the hour. Rather, it is clear that it is asked, impatiently in reiteration, because the questioner is waiting for the morning. In the interpretation I dare to give here, it would also be clear what that morning is: the dawn when God will reappear in dazzling majesty over the hills of that desert landscape. When will this morning finally come? The pathos of the little dialogue comes from the simple reply of the watchman: He doesn't know.

We are many centuries removed from even the most recent time when this song could have been composed or introduced into the canon of the Hebrew prophets. Yet if we understand it in the way I have suggested, it suddenly has meaning for us too. Our situation is vastly different from that of the Jewish people in the centuries between the Babylonian exile and the period of Jesus. The pluralistic dynamic that has been discussed at great length in this book points up, all by itself, how great that difference is. But we too wait in the darkness for the dawn of God's morning.

Watchmen are mentioned several times in the Hebrew Bible, both literally and metaphorically. In another part of the Book of Isaiah, in the fifty-second chapter which very likely belongs to the powerful voice of Deutero-Isaiah in the mid-sixth century, when most of Israel was exiled in Babylonia, watchmen are called upon to proclaim the return of God in glory:

> *How beautiful upon the mountains*
> *are the feet of him who brings good tidings,*
> *who publishes peace, who brings good tidings of good,*
> *who publishes salvation,*
> *who says to Zion, "Your God reigns."*

> *Hark, your watchmen lift up their voice,*
> *together they sing for joy;*
> *for eye to eye they see*
> *the return of the Lord to Zion.*

We too have our "watchmen" today. Some pretend to know what time it is in our night of waiting; but it invariably turns out to be the wrong time. Others, even worse, try to convince us that there is nothing to wait for, that the night in which we find ourselves is all there is, that in effect God's morning will never come. We also have honest watchmen, like the one who made his rounds in long-ago Se'ir, who tell us that they do not know. Now as then, this is a discouraging reply. Our short text, though, ends on a note of hope: Come back and ask again, for the morning *will* come. The burden of God's silence will be lifted and He will return once more in the dawn, "with flaming fire at his right hand," in the fullness of His glory.